LITTLE BOOK OF
LAND SPEED RECORDS

Liam McCann

LITTLE BOOK OF
LAND SPEED RECORDS

First published in the UK in 2015

© Demand Media Limited 2015

www.demand-media.co.uk

Printed and bound in Europe

ISBN 978-1-910540-44-2

Contents

The Future of the Land Speed Record...

Introduction

In 1886 German engineer Karl Benz invented a petrol-powered automobile that became the first production motor vehicle. Steam and electric cars already existed but they were slow and cumbersome, and the internal-combustion engine revolutionised the industry. Only a decade or so later, drivers of all three types of car were battling for the outright speed record.

The first person to hold the official land speed record was Count Gaston de Chasseloup-Laubat. He took his electric car to Agricole Park just outside Paris in December 1898 and recorded a speed of 39.24mph over a flying kilometre. There was great concern for his health as drivers were expected to suffer heart failure or be unable to breathe at such speeds. Five months later, Camille Jenatzy raised the record to 65.70mph, the first time that a car had travelled at more than a mile a minute.

The rules governing record-breaking

still hadn't been formalised so brave runs of 63.10 to 84.73mph by Charles Rolls, and several high-speed attempts – of which the fastest was at 76.08mph by American William Kissam Vander-bilt – weren't officially recognised. (This book includes a selection of the unoffi-cial records, although it is by no means exhaustive as the various clubs and gov-erning bodies didn't agree on a complete set of rules until 1964.)

It wasn't until 1904 that 100mph was reached over the flying kilometre when Frenchman Louis Rigolly took his 100-horsepower Gobron-Brillié onto the beach at Ostend in Belgium. Two years later, American Fred Marriott took his steam-powered car onto the road course at Daytona Beach and ex-ceeded two miles a minute for the first time. The next milestone – 150mph over a two-way run – fell to one of the great-est names in the history of land speed re-cord-breaking: Sir Malcolm Campbell.

Campbell was almost denied the glory, however, as prodigiously talented Italian-American Indy Car racer Ralph DePalma made an attempt on the speed

ABOVE Charles Rolls competes in the 1906 Tourist Trophy

record in a Packard at Daytona Beach in 1919. DePalma had a glittering career but he'd almost been killed when he was impaled by a corn stalk having crashed during a road race in Milwaukee in 1912. He spent 11 weeks in hospital but recovered to take the 1914 Vanderbilt Cup and the 1915 Indy 500. He then drove the Packard at 149.86mph along the sands at Daytona but he didn't make a return run to qualify for an outright record. Although some details

LEFT Louis Rigolly prepares for a record attempt along the beach at Ostend

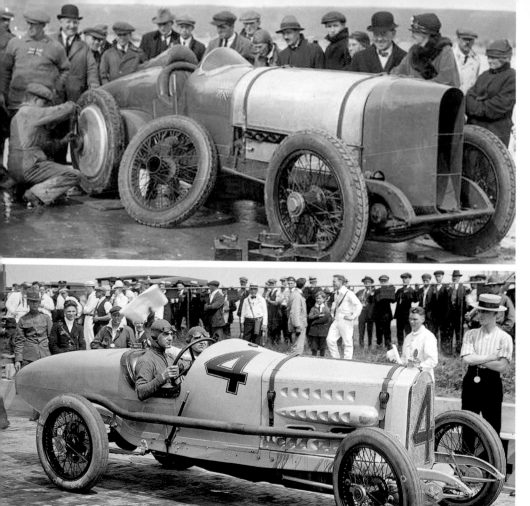

OPPOSITE TOP
Malcolm Campbell's 350hp Sunbeam is prepared for a crack at the record on Pendine Sands

OPPOSITE BOTTOM
The incomparable Ralph DePalma

LEFT Kenelm Lee Guinness at the 1914 French Grand Prix

of his life remain sketchy, DePalma was undoubtedly one of the greatest drivers of his or indeed any era. His record of leading 612 laps at the Indy 500 wasn't broken until Al Unser won the 1987 event. And in his Associated Press obituary, DePalma was said to have competed in 2,889 races in a career spanning 27 years. That he won 2,557 remains one of the most impressive starts-to-wins ratios in all professional sport.

The war slowed the progression of the outright record but Malcolm Campbell took a 350-horsepower V12 Sunbeam onto Pendine Sands in Carmarthen-shire in March 1925 and registered a speed of 150.87mph. It should be noted that American Tommy Milton had run a Duesenberg along Daytona Beach at 156.03mph in 1920 but, like DePalma, he'd also only run in one direction so the record was unofficial.

Campbell had to fend off more competition in the shape of Irishman Kenelm Lee Guinness, a former road racer at the Isle of Man TT who had then invented

the KLG sparkplug. Guinness used the same V12 Sunbeam to reach 133.75mph in 1922 but he crashed two years later and retired from record-breaking. Next in line to try to claim Campbell's record was Sir Henry Segrave, a dashing Grand Prix driver in the sport's golden age. He won several GPs on the continent and then took the land speed record from Campbell with a 152.33mph run in 1926. The following year he reclaimed it from Campbell with the first 200mph record in a 1,000-horsepower twin-engined Sunbeam at Daytona. Welsh-man Parry Thomas raised the record in a Higham Special on Pendine Sands but he was killed during another attempt when his driving chain broke loose.

Despite the obvious dangers, this was a glorious era for record-breaking, but the British didn't have a monopoly on the cutting-edge cars in the late 1920s. American Ray Keech built a monstrous 81-litre triple-engined White Triplex record-breaker called *Spirit of Elkdom*. In April 1928, this behemoth roared down Daytona Beach at 207.55mph to set a new land speed record. Segrave reclaimed the title the following year so Triplex owner Jim White asked Keech to have another crack at the record. Keech

realised the car was running at its limit so wisely refused, but the team's mechanic, Lee Bible, agreed to drive the car. His first run was slow but the return yielded a speed of just over 200mph. During deceleration, Bible lost control and the car crashed into the dunes, throwing him to his death before rolling into and killing photographer Charles Traub. The dangers were increasing as rapidly as the speeds but that didn't stop teams from trying to raise the record further.

Countryman Frank Lockhart used ice to cool the three-litre Miller engine in his Stutz *Black Hawk Special* in 1928. The winner of the 1926 Indianapolis 500 overshot and ended up in the sea on his first run and the Stutz then lost a tyre on a later pass at more than 200mph. The car flew out of control, killing Lockhart instantly.

The British pair of Campbell and Segrave traded records for the next five years but it was Campbell who was the first man to reach 250mph when he took one of his *Blue Bird* cars with

OPPOSITE Henry Segrave prepares for the 1921 French Grand Prix

ABOVE The burnt-out wreck of John Parry-Thomas's record-breaking Babs

ABOVE The world was reminded of the dangers of chasing the land speed record when Lee Bible was killed in the White Triplex at Daytona Beach in 1928

a supercharged Napier Lion engine to 253.97mph at Daytona in 1933. For the next two years, Campbell obliterated the record and threatened to take it out of reach for decades. By 1935, he'd become the first man to reach 300mph, although the Daytona Beach track was now too short for safe runs so Campbell took the Rolls-Royce aero-engined *Blue*

Bird to what would become the home of land speed record-breaking: the Bonneville Salt Flats in Utah. The 4,000-foot altitude reduced the car's power by around 15% from a claimed 2,500bhp but Campbell still managed to raise the record to 301.13mph. This was the great man's last land speed record, although his son Donald continued the family

name and the fabulous *Bluebird* line of cars and boats.

Three years later, John Cobb averaged 350.20mph in the *Railton Mobil Special* on the salt flats, but there were very few record attempts over the next nine years as the world had been plunged into another war. Although Cobb raised the outright record to 394.20mph in 1947 (with one run at 403mph), it was 16 years before another serious attempt was made. By then, American Athol Graham had already been killed when his *City of Salt Lake* car crashed at Bonneville in August 1960. Donald Campbell was then lucky to survive a 325mph crash

ABOVE Frank Lockhart at the wheel of the beautiful Black Hawk

LEFT Lockhart was also killed in a record attempt

in *Bluebird*, while Art Arfons, Nathan Ostich and Mickey Thompson all failed to capture the outright record. Mickey Thompson was particularly unlucky as he managed to coax *Challenger 1* up to 407mph on one run but a driveshaft failure prevented him from making a return run within the hour stipulated by the governing body.

In the 1960s, American hot-rodders started experimenting with jet cars on the salt flats. The rules governing record attempts didn't allow for such vehicles as they often didn't have four wheels that were driven by the engine but that didn't stop Craig Breedlove building a free-wheeling tricycle called *Spirit of America* and equipping it with a General Electric J47 turbojet. In August 1963, Breedlove

registered a two-way average speed of 407.45mph, and the record was accepted by the Fédération Internationale de Motocyclisme (FIM) rather than the Fédération Internationale de l'Automobile. By the end of the following year, the FIA had amended the rules to allow jet cars, although they insisted that these vehicles should have four wheels if they were to claim the outright record.

This ushered in two decades of competition amongst the Americans, although Donald Campbell did manage a solitary record for the British in 1964 when he took his Bluebird-Proteus onto Lake Eyre in Australia. His 403.10mph run was one of the last of the piston-engined wheel-driven records. Thereafter, only specialist rocket- or jet-powered

vehicles have held the outright record.

With the British challenge fading after Campbell decided to concentrate on the water speed record, the only pressure on Breedlove came from Walt Arfons with his car, *Wingfoot Express*, and Walt's brother Art with his *Green Monster* jet car. The trio battled it out on the salt flats and between them they raised the record to 600.60mph when Breedlove's *Spirit of America Sonic 1* blasted down the track in November 1965. This record stood for

five years until North American Aviation employee and Apollo test astronaut Gary Gabelich took the Natural Gas Industry's *Blue Flame* rocket car onto the salt flats and recorded a new record at 630.38mph.

The cost of running a team on the flats and the danger involved when the speeds were so great combined to prohibit record attempts for most of the 1970s. Towards the end of the decade, however, a British team decided to try to recapture the title. While they were

ABOVE John Cobb's Railton Mobil Special raised the record to 394mph

RIGHT Mickey Thompson's Challenger 1 almost reclaimed the record for the United States

BELOW Craig Breedlove's original Spirit of America

promoting the project and raising sponsorship – businessman Richard Noble famously started out with only £175 – an American team under stuntman and film director Hal Needham decided to aim beyond the record and shoot for the sound barrier instead. Noble, it seemed, was going to lose out to American corporate muscle. Needham and driver Stan Barrett then built the most controversial car in the history of record-breaking: the *Budweiser Rocket*.

The three-wheeled car was designed by William Fredrick and resembled the *Blue Flame* in that it was a sleek hybrid rocket-powered vehicle that also used the propulsion system from a Sidewinder missile to provide extra boost. It first ran at Bonneville in 1976 but the team immediately realised it didn't have enough power to maintain a record speed through the measured mile. They therefore decided that they would try to break the sound barrier instead as this only needed a peak top speed and didn't require the team to

BELOW The Green Monster team at Bonneville in 1964

Thrust 2 broke several British records on RAF runways in 1980 so the team relocated to Bonneville in 1981. The weather was appalling, however, and the record attempt had to be postponed until the following year. Conditions were equally bad in 1982 so the team desperately looked for an alternative track. A chance conversation led them to the Black Rock Desert in Nevada but time was short and Noble only managed to reach 590.55mph, 32mph short of Gabelich's flying-mile record. In 1983, their luck changed and *Thrust 2* became one of the only land speed cars to reach its design speed of 650mph. Running in opposite directions within the allotted hour, Noble reclaimed the record for Britain with a new record average of 633.47mph.

In the 1990s, three teams entered the race to record the first official supersonic land speed record. McGlashan was back with *Aussie Invader II*, a 36,000 horsepower brute propelled by the jet turbine from a Mirage fighter; Noble and RAF pilot Andy Green were developing *Thrust SSC*, which had two Rolls-Royce

turn the car round for a second run in the opposite direction. This, of course, meant that the governing body wouldn't ratify any record.

In December 1979 Barrett drove the car at Rogers Dry Lake. And there the controversy starts. The team claimed the car had gone supersonic and that air force radar equipment and their own telemetry proved it. However, they have never released their data and no sonic boom was heard. As the run was inconclusive, Noble's *Thrust 2* was now the frontrunner to reclaim the outright record.

Australian Rosco McGlashan briefly thought about entering the race with his jet-powered *Aussie Invader* dragster but his project eventually faltered. By then, Noble's team had the budget and technical nous to build a serious contender.

jet turbofans; and Craig Breedlove had built a new *Spirit of America*. The indomitable Aussie was the first to have a crack at Noble's record. In 1993 he took the car onto the salt flats of Lake Gairdner in Australia but bad weather limited him to 450mph. The following year the salt was still in poor condition and McGlashan crashed at 580mph. *Aussie Invader II* struck the timing equipment 200 yards from the track and was destroyed. McGlashan, thankfully, walked away with only dented pride and immediately began developing *Aussie Invader III*.

Breedlove arrived at the Black Rock Desert in 1996, a year before Noble was ready to unleash *Thrust SSC*. The American had the advantage and he looked set to take the record when his *Spirit of America Formula Shell* was thrown on its side by a crosswind at 675mph. Breedlove managed to regain a small measure of control but the car was badly damaged and the team were forced to postpone their attempt for another season. This gave McGlashan a brief opportunity to steal the record in *Aussie Invader III* towards the end of the year. His team returned to Lake Gairdner and immediately began making fast test runs. McGlashan then recorded a peak speed of 638mph, a shade faster than *Thrust 2*'s average over the two runs. To claim an official record, McGlashan needed to make a return run within an hour but the weather conspired against him and *Thrust 2*'s record remained intact.

By 1997, Noble was ready and Breedlove had repaired *Spirit of*

BELOW The Budweiser Rocket remains the most controversial car in the history of the land speed record

America so the two teams faced off at Black Rock Desert. Breedlove suffered engine trouble early in the duel, which handed the advantage to Noble and driver Andy Green. When *Thrust SSC* set a new record of 714mph, Breedlove realised that the record was probably out of reach, although he did make a 676mph pass in the repaired *Spirit of America*. More technical problems prohibited the car from running near

its design maximum of 800mph and, when Green blasted down the playa at 763mph on October 15, 1997, the first ever sonic boom generated by a land speed car echoed across the desert. This supersonic record raised the bar and effectively ended the contest.

Several teams are now vying to set a new land speed record but their budgets, technical know-how and preparation are a far cry from where it all began.

Chapter 2

Gaston de Chasseloup-Laubat

Born: 1867, Paris, France | **Died:** November 20, 1903, Paris, France

Count Gaston de Chasseloup-Laubat was a French racing driver who won the prestigious long-distance Marseille-La Turbie road-race in a steam-powered car in 1897. The 140-mile (220km) event was part of Nice Speed Week and took the competitors along a primitive coastal road to the village in the hills above Monaco near the Italian border.

OPPOSITE Gaston de Chasseloup-Laubat in the Jeantaud Duc

The following year, Chasseloup-Laubat entered a competition sponsored by *La France Automobile* magazine to find the fastest car-and-driver combination on Earth. Chasseloup-Laubat approached car manufacturer Jeantaud and they provided him with an electric Duc for the record attempt. In December 1898, he completed the one-kilometre course in 57 seconds at an average speed of 39.24mph. Over the next three months, he and rival Camille Jenatzy traded speed records but it was Jenatzy who had the final say with a 65.79mph run that lasted three years.

Count Gaston de Chasseloup-Laubat died in Paris at the age of just 36.

RECORDS

Date	Venue	Car	Speed
December 18, 1898	Achères, France	Jeantaud Duc	39.24mph / 63.15kph
January 17, 1899	Achères, France	Jeantaud Duc	41.41mph / 66.64kph
March 4, 1899	Achères, France	Jeantaud Duc	57.65mph / 92.78kph

Chapter 3

Camille Jenatzy

Born: 1868, Schaerbeek, Belgium | **Died:** December 8, 1913, Habay La Neuve, Luxemburg

Camille Jenatzy was a Belgian racer who earned the nickname The Red Devil on account of his flowing beard.

He enjoyed a great rivalry with Gaston de Chasseloup-Laubat, with the pair trading land speed records for the first four months of 1899. Jenatzy might have conceded defeat when Gaston de Chasseloup-Laubat reached nearly 60mph in March but he modified a specially designed electric car and became the first man to travel at more than a mile a minute at the end of April. Jenatzy held the record for three years but he contin-ued racing cars and took the prestigious 1903 Gordon Bennett Cup in Ireland at the wheel of a Mercedes. He then predicted that he would die in the same make of car.

His prediction came true 10 years later when he was out hunting with friends in the forests of Luxemburg. He hid behind a tree and pretended to be an animal to wind them up but Alfred Madoux fell for the prank and fired. Jenatzy was rushed to hospital but he bled to death in the Mercedes before doctors could treat him. He was buried in Brussels.

OPPOSITE Camille Jenatzy in the Jamais Contente immediately after his record run in April 1899

RECORDS

Date	Venue	Car	Speed
January 17, 1899	Achères, France	CGA Dogcart	41.42mph / 66.66kph
January 27, 1899	Achères, France	CGA Dogcart	49.93mph / 80.35kph
April 29, 1899	Achères, France	CITA *La Jamais Contente*	65.79mph / 105.88kph

Chapter 4

Léon Serpollet

Born: October 4, 1858, Culoz, France | **Died:** February 1, 1907, Paris, France

Léon Serpollet was born in the Ain department of Bourg-en-Bresse in eastern France. He eventually moved to Paris and established an engineering factory on the Rue des Cloÿs.

He began by making three-wheeled steam carriages that could reach speeds of more than 20mph. In 1894, four of his early horseless carriages competed in the Paris-Rouen race, although two cars failed to finish and the others could only manage 14th and 16th.

OPPOSITE Léon Serpollet in the Easter Egg

By 1896 he'd perfected the design of a flash boiler that enabled steam engines to be used in cars. He then used this new technology to redesign outdated steam locomotives for the French railways. In 1902, Serpollet modified a car that he had built and American industrialist Frank Gardner had financed. He took the steam-powered vehicle, nicknamed *Easter Egg*, onto the Promenade des Anglais in Nice and reached more than 75mph over the flying kilometre. He died in Paris in 1907 at the age of 48.

RECORD

Date	Venue	Car	Speed
April 13, 1902	Nice, France	Gardner-Serpollet	75.06mph / 120.80kph

Chapter 5

William Kissam 'Willie K' Vanderbilt II

Born: March 2, 1878, New York, USA | **Died:** January 8, 1944, New York

Willie K was born into a wealthy American railroad family (his father inherited $55 million – approximately $1.5 billion today – from his father, William Henry Vanderbilt). Vanderbilt Senior moved into the family business but he also bred racehorses and helped found the Jockey Club. In 1879 he bought P.T. Barnum's Great Roman Hippodrome and renamed the venue Madison Square Garden. He also co-owned the yacht Defender, which won the America's Cup in 1895.

He clearly passed a love of speed onto his son, Willie K, and Vanderbilt Junior soon headed to the Mors automobile company in France to challenge the Europeans. Road racing was the preserve of Mors and Panhard-Levassor but

RIGHT William Kissam Vanderbilt II was born into a wealthy railroad family

OPPOSITE Willie K at the wheel of the 90-horsepower Mercedes he drove to a land speed record in 1904

Vanderbilt had his eyes on the land speed record and Mors's new internal-combustion-engine-powered machines were tipped to usurp the electric and steam-powered vehicles of the previous century.

Émile Mors delivered him a 60-horsepower grand prix car with a 9.2-litre V4 engine that had a steel chassis and four-speed transmission driving the rear wheels. With minor modifications, Willie K took the machine up to a shade over 76mph in 1902 but this was a busy year for record-breaking and Henry Fournier and compatriot Georges Augières raised it to 77.13mph later in November. The following year, Charles Rolls also raced a modified Mors to two more records, and by 1904 it stood at 84.73mph.

Willie K headed back to the US and took a 90-horsepower Mercedes onto Daytona Beach to try to reclaim the record for America. In January 1904 he covered a flying mile in 39 seconds at 92.30mph but the racing establishment in Europe didn't ratify his mark. Instead, it was hailed as an absolute record for land vehicles in America. Such was Willie's passion for motorsport that he then established the Vanderbilt Cup, the first and most prestigious trophy presented for racing in North America.

He served in the naval reserve during the First World War and died of heart failure aged 65.

RECORDS

Date	Venue	Car	Speed
November 5, 1902	Albis-Saint Arnoult, France	Mors	76.08mph / 122.44kph
January 28, 1904	Daytona Beach, USA	Mercedes	92.30mph / 148.54kph

Chapter 6

Henry Ford

Born: July 30, 1863, Michigan, USA | **Died:** April 7, 1947, Michigan, USA

Henry Ford was an American industrialist who saw the potential of the automobile and realised it could be mass-produced on production lines. This would make it cheap, reliable and accessible to ordinary people. He therefore transformed the image of the motorcar from elitist curiosity to ubiquitous essential.

His father wanted him to run the family farm but Ford had loftier ambitions and moved to Detroit in 1879 at the age of 16. He learned how to service steam engines and was soon chief engineer at Thomas Edison's light-bulb company. Edison convinced him to move into car manufacture and he'd established the Henry Ford Company by 1901. Ford left the company after Henry Leland's

arrival in 1902 but he continued designing cars and had soon built an 80-horsepower Ford 999 racer. Despite its initial success, Ford continued to struggle to find investors but he eventually secured financial backing from Alex Malcomson and the Dodge brothers and they founded the Ford Motor Company in June 1903.

Ford had to raise the company's profile so he took a modified 999 onto the frozen Lake St Clair between Ontario and Michigan and set a new land speed record of 91.37mph. He then hired racing driver Barney Oldfield to drive the car around the country to secure more investment. The record might have fallen (unofficially) to Vanderbilt the following month but the plan worked and Ford was producing the landmark

Model T by 1908. Ten years later, half of all the cars in North America were Model Ts, and, when production ceased in 1927, more than 15 million had been produced (a record that would last for 45 years). Due to the long-running confusion over the rules governing the land speed record, Ford's effort wasn't ini-

Date	Venue	Car	Speed
January 12, 1904	Lake St Clair, USA	Ford 999	91.37mph / 147.05kph

tially recognised by the Fédération Internationale de l'Automobile but it has since been reinstated.

Ford championed the League of Nations to safeguard peace at the end of the First World War, he also introduced a $5 working day (doubling the salary of most of his staff), and he ran such a tight ship that his company was never audited while he was at the helm. However, despite hiring black workers alongside disabled workers and women, Ford inexplicably expressed fierce anti-Semitic sentiments in his book *The International Jew: the World's Foremost Problem*, and he also maintained contacts and contracts with Nazi Germany. He died of a brain haemorrhage in 1947.

OPPOSITE Henry Ford with driver Barney Oldfield in 1902

BELOW William Clay at the wheel of a Ford 999 in 1953

Chapter 7

Louis Rigolly

Born: March 1, 1876, Chamesson, France | **Died:** January 7, 1958, Seine-Maritime, France

In May 1903 Belgian driver Pierre de Caters drove a DMG Mercedes Simplex at 97.25mph over a one-kilometre course on a beach near Ostend.

Five years later he became the first Belgian to fly an aircraft. The 100mph barrier eluded him in both forms of transport, however, and it was Frenchman Louis Rigolly who became the first to three figures on land. Rigolly had come close early in 1904 when he took a monstrous 13.5-litre

OPPOSITE Louis Rigolly before the 1904 French Grand Prix

Gobron-Brillié along the Promenade des Anglais in Nice at 94.78mph, but he then returned to Ostend and made several minor modifications to the car's streamlining.

Rigolly roared down the sand at nearly 104mph in the summer of 1904, but his record only stood for three months before it fell to Paul Baras in a Darracq on the same beach. (Rigolly also scored notable victories across the continent in his 110-horsepower machine.) Baras only held the record for a few months

RECORDS

Date	Venue	Car	Speed
March 31, 1904	Nice, France	Gobron-Brillié	94.78mph / 152.53kph
July 21, 1904	Ostend, Belgium	Gobron-Brillié	103.56mph / 166.66kph

as Arthur MacDonald soon took it in a six-cylinder Napier. Victor Hémery then reclaimed the record for France in a Darracq.

Chapter 8

Fred Marriott

Born: December 31, 1872, Massachusetts, USA | **Died:** April 28, 1956, USA

Fred Marriott was an American racing driver who took a steam-powered *Stanley* car onto the Daytona Beach road course in January 1906. Having reached nearly 128mph, he claimed the world land speed record and the Stanley twins who'd built the car were awarded the Dewar Trophy.

The latter was bequeathed by British MP Sir Thomas Dewar on the condition that it be awarded annually to the car or driver whose achievements helped further the interests of the motor industry. The re-cord was the first to exceed 200kph and two miles per minute, and it also marked the first time that the record for a car had surpassed that of a train.

The rules governing the land speed record were constantly evolving in this period as cars could be steam-, battery- or internal-combustion-powered. Some records were recognised by the administrative FIA while others were not, and some were later reinstated as the rules evolved further. As several categories were introduced to resolve the confusion, the record went up and

RECORD

Date	Venue	Car	Speed
January 26, 1906	Ormond Beach, USA	*Stanley Steamer*	127.66mph / 205.44kph

down several times in the early part of the 20th century.

Marriott took the steamer onto Daytona Beach the following year but he hit a rut while travelling at around 150mph and the car took to the air before crashing heavily. He was injured in the impact and retired from record-breaking

with immediate effect. His outright record lasted until 1924, by which time petrol engines were delivering far more power. His record for a steam-powered vehicle wasn't beaten until Charles Burnett took the *Inspiration* to 139.84mph (225.06kph) at Edwards Air Force Base in California in 2009.

ABOVE Fred Marriott in the Stanley Steamer in 1907

Chapter 9

Victor Hémery

Born: November 18, 1876, Sarthe, France | **Died:** September 9, 1950, Le Mans, France

Victor Hémery joined car manufacturer Darracq as their chief test driver in 1904. The Gordon Bennett Series was still the most prestigious event in Europe so he helped prepare their cars, and he also drove an Open-Darracq to victory in the Hamburg-Bahrenfeld road race. In 1905 he won in the Ardennes in Belgium and also took the Vanderbilt Cup in the USA. He then set an unofficial land speed record at nearly 110mph.

Having made a name for himself as a superb driver in a heroic age of motorsport, he defected to Benz in 1907 and won the St Petersburg-Moscow road race in appalling conditions. He backed this up with podium finishes at the French and US Grand Prix. Two years later he set an official land speed record of 125.94mph at the Brooklands race track in Surrey at the wheel of a Blitzen (lightning) Benz. He then helped the team to a 1-2 finish at the 1910 US

RECORDS

Date	Venue	Car	Speed
December 30, 1905	Arles, France	Darracq	109.65mph / 176.46kph
November 8, 1909	Brooklands, United Kingdom	Benz No.1	125.94mph / 202.68kph

Grand Prix. His final win came in a FIAT S61 in 1911 at the French Grand Prix on his home track. He died in 1950 but was retroactively awarded the 1905 North American Drivers' Championship the following year.

ABOVE Victor Hémery before the 1905 Vanderbilt Cup, a race he went on to win

Chapter 10

Lydston Granville Hornsted

Born: 1884, Moscow, Russia | **Died:** 1957, London, England

Hornsted was born in Russia to a British diplomat and his wife, but he eventually returned to Britain and worked as a motor mechanic.

Just before Christmas 1913, Hornsted took a 200-horsepower Benz out at Brooklands in Surrey and broke two world records, the first over half a mile (70.71mph / 113.8kph) and the second over a kilometre (73.82mph / 118.8kph), both of which were from a standing start. He then asked the car's manufacturers in Mannheim whether

OPPOSITE Lydston Hornsted prepares for a record attempt in a Blitzen Benz at Brooklands

they could modify it for an assault on the world land speed record.

The German engineers modified the radiator grille, added a wind deflector and extended the exhaust from the enormous 21.5-litre engine to the rear of the car with a stovepipe. He broke more records over two miles and five miles in January 1914, but the FIA changed the rules again so that any attempt on the outright speed record had to be made in both directions to allow for variations in gradient and wind. The average speed over the two runs would then be taken

RECORD

Date	Venue	Car	Speed
June 24, 1914	Brooklands, United Kingdom	Blitzen Benz	124.12mph / 199.71kph

as the car's final speed. Hornsted blasted down the straight at Brooklands at an average speed of 124mph to set a new two-way world record.

Chapter 11

Ernest Arthur Douglas Eldridge

Born: July 18, 1897, Hampstead, London, England | **Died:** October 27, 1937, Kensington, London

Ernest Eldridge was born into a wealthy family and attended Harrow School. However, he left the school in the sixth form to fight on the Western Front during the Great War. He immediately joined the Red Cross and served as an ambulance driver and with the French artillery.

After the war, he trained as an engineer at Brooklands in Surrey and soon became bitten by the speed bug. He qualified as a pilot in 1923 but then devoted his attention to cramming enormous aero engines into small Italian chassis in the pursuit of records.

He caused something of a stir when he fitted a little Isotta-Fraschini with a 20-litre 240-horsepower Maybach aero-plane engine and then lapped the famous circuit at more than 100mph. When he sold the car, he invested the money in a 10-litre FIAT and was so successful that he was able to buy another car with his winnings. He christened the new FIAT *Mephistopheles* and fitted it with a massive 21.7-litre 350-horsepower engine. He immediately set a world record for the half-mile from a standing start (23.17 seconds / 77.68mph), so he then took the car to France for an assault on the land speed record, which had recently been raised to 143.31mph by Frenchman René Thomas in a 280-horsepower V12 Delage designed by Charles Planchon.

In July 1924, Eldridge gunned the monstrous *Mephistopheles* along a

straight stretch of road (this was the last such attempt on public highways) and reached 146mph over the flying kilometre. Three months later, he set an endurance record by covering 210 kilometres in one hour at the Montlhéry circuit just south of Paris. He gave up chasing records the following year and embarked on a grand prix career instead.

Having raced at the Brooklands 200

ABOVE A signed photo of Ernest Eldridge before his record run in the FIAT Mephistopheles at Arpajon

and Indy 500 he returned to Europe to try for more endurance records at Montlhéry. During one attempt, his front axle collapsed and Eldridge was thrown from the car as it somersaulted. He suffered severe head injuries and lost an eye, which forced him to retire from record-breaking. He decided to manage Captain George Eyston instead, as the engineer and inventor went for speed and endurance records in an MG EX-120. Eldridge also helped Eyston design a Roll-Royce-engined record car called *Speed of the Wind*.

While returning from a trip to Bonneville, Eldridge contracted pneumonia. When he died in Kensington in 1937 at the age of 40, the world lost a pioneering racer and one of the land speed record's most colourful characters – he was rumoured to have blown most of the family fortune on racing and once lost £60,000 on the turn of a card while gambling in the Casino de Monte Carlo.

RECORD			
Date	**Venue**	**Car**	**Speed**
July 12, 1924	Arpajon, Paris, France	FIAT *Mephistopheles*	146.01mph / 234.98kph

Chapter 12

Sir Malcolm Campbell

Born: March 11, 1885, Chislehurst, Kent, England | **Died:** December 31, 1948, Reigate, Surrey, England

Sir Malcolm Campbell is perhaps the greatest record-breaker of them all. He was the only son of a diamond trader and went to Uppingham School. He then went to Germany to learn the diamond trade but ended up developing a fascination with motorcycle racing. When he returned to London, he worked on very low pay for three years and concentrated instead on winning motorbike races between London and Lakes End. By 1910 he was racing cars at Brooklands and, having seen the play *The Blue Bird,* decided to christen all of his cars by that name.

Racing at Brooklands was interrupted by the war, so Campbell took to the skies with the Royal Flying Corps. At the end of the war he decided to pursue his fas-

cination with speed on land and water. In 1922 he returned to Brooklands and borrowed Kenelm Lee Guinness's Sunbeam after the Irishman had set a land speed record of 133.75mph at the track. Campbell modified the car and installed an 18.3-litre 350-horsepower V12 aero engine that had four blocks of three cylinders arranged in two banks set at 60 degrees. Each cylinder had one inlet and two exhaust valves actuated by a single overhead camshaft. The camshafts were driven by a set of 16 gears from the front of the crankshaft. A four-speed transmission drove the rear axle with a differential driveshaft rather than the hazardous chains used by other record-breaking cars. Campbell then added a streamlined nose cowling and a pointed tail to reduce drag. He also upgraded the rear drum brakes and damped shock absorbers.

Campbell first drove the car in 1922 and reached a speed of 138.08mph but it didn't count as a record because the track used a manual timing system. He then travelled to Denmark and registered 137.72mph but the timing equipment was also deemed substandard so the

record remained out of reach. Campbell made more aerodynamic modifications the following year and returned to the beach at Fanø in Denmark for another crack at the land speed record. A large crowd had gathered to cheer him on but the beach was in poor condition and the tyres couldn't cope with the surface. On one run, *Blue Bird* narrowly missed the spectators so Campbell refused to make another attempt unless the officials moved the crowd back. Sadly, they ignored him and when a tyre exploded

BELOW Campbell in the Napier Blue Bird II at Pendine Sands in 1927

on his next run its remains flew into the crowd and killed a young boy.

Campbell decided that Pendine Sands on the south coast of Wales was a safer venue as the seven-mile beach was usually deserted. In September 1924, he finally set his first official land speed record at 146.16mph. It was the beginning of an 11-year association with the record that remains unsurpassed. He wanted to sell *Blue Bird* to fund his racing team at Brooklands but he decided to keep the car when he heard that Welsh engineer and part-time racing driver John Parry-Thomas wanted a tilt at the title in a Higham Special. Campbell returned to Pendine the following summer and raised the record to 150.87mph, which he hoped was beyond Parry-Thomas's reach. (The Sunbeam was returned to racing trim and competed at Brooklands until at least 1936. It was then sold to the Beaulieu Motor Museum in 1958, where it remains to this day.)

It took Campbell and his mechanics two years before they were ready for another assault on the record. Henry Segrave and Parry-Thomas had both broken it in 1926 and the mark now stood at 171.02mph so Campbell asked aeronautical engineer Charles Amherst

Villiers and his usual mechanic, Leo Villa, to build him a W12 500-horse-power successor to the Sunbeam. They used a Napier Lion aero engine to reach Campbell's target of 200mph but the first run at Pendine (with the wind in his favour) only yielded 195mph. The return was much slower, although he did claim the outright record average at 174.88mph.

Campbell may have broken the record but he was disappointed with the car's performance and Segrave pounced later in the year when he took a 900-horsepower Sunbeam to Daytona. The car must have surprised Campbell as Segrave posted a speed of 203.79mph, thereby becoming the first team to break three miles per minute as well. Campbell became even more agitated when Segrave was knighted for his achievement and he vowed to reclaim the record.

He spent the next winter rebuilding *Blue Bird II* and convinced the air ministry to lend him a 900-horsepower sprint engine from a Schneider Trophy Supermarine seaplane. Designer Rex Pierson even borrowed aircraft manufacturer Vickers's wind tunnel to fine-tune the car's aerodynamics. Having reviewed the data, he moved

ABOVE Blue Bird III

the radiators back and mounted them externally so that a streamlined nose could be added. He also insisted on a central tailfin to increase stability. In 1928, *Blue Bird III* roared along Daytona Beach at 206.96mph and the record was Campbell's once more. However, only two months later, Ray Keech stole the record back for America with his outrageous 81-litre White Triplex.

Campbell knew his car in its current configuration wasn't capable of much more and he was also concerned that a tidal beach was too unpredictable a

ABOVE Campbell with Blue Bird III at Daytona Beach

OPPOSITE Campbell at the wheel of the latest incarnation of Blue Bird in 1932

venue so he began scouting for alternatives. He eventually settled on a dry lakebed in South Africa but, having seen no rain for five years, the area was suddenly swamped after unseasonal storms. It had been a fruitless trip: Campbell had lost his briefcase, survived a plane crash when his light aircraft hit a tree near Calvinia, and avoided puff adders and scorpions while clearing a 16-mile track, but the rain then washed out his record attempt. When Campbell returned to Cape Town he was dealt another blow when he learned that Segrave had raised the record to 231.44 mph. *Blue Bird* now needed to be completely rebuilt, and the result was a 23.9-litre W12 1,450-horsepower supercharged Campbell-Napier-

ABOVE Sir Malcolm with son Donald in around 1934

Railton. This enormous car was 25 feet (7.60m) long and weighed nearly four tonnes.

With conditions in South Africa too unpredictable, Campbell returned to Daytona in 1931. Segrave had been killed while trying for a water speed record so there was less pressure from a British rival. The Americans, however, also had eyes on the prize so Campbell decided to take it out of their reach with a series of cars. He first raised the record to 246.09mph and was knighted on his return to Britain. He revisited Daytona three more times in various incarnations of *Blue Bird*, raising the record to

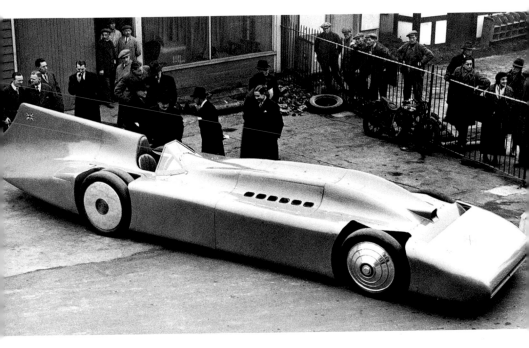

253.97mph in 1932; 272.46mph in 1933; and 276.82mph in 1935.

The 1933 Campbell-Railton boasted a 36.7-litre supercharged Rolls-Royce R V12 engine delivering 2,300 horse-power. Although Campbell smashed the record, the car was up to 50mph short of its potential because the tyres couldn't provide enough grip on the sand. Two years later, the car had been largely redesigned and sported a longer tailfin. Two extra tyres were mounted on the rear to increase traction, and airbrakes were added for safety, but the sand was uneven in places and the car still didn't reach its potential. Campbell needed to find a venue where he could finally exploit the car's power, and he eventually chose the Bonneville Salt Flats in Utah. In the last run of his incredible career, Sir Malcolm Campbell became the first man in history to drive at more than 300mph. In so doing, he raised the two-way average to a new land speed record of 301.13mph.

Thereafter, Campbell concentrated on the water speed record. He reclaimed the title from the Americans in 1937 when he took *Blue Bird K3* to 126.33mph at Lake Maggiore. He knew that building a faster boat would take the record out of sight so he commissioned a three-point hydroplane and christened the new machine *Blue Bird K4*. Just before the outbreak of the Second World War, Campbell set his fourth and final water speed record with a run of 141.74mph on Coniston Water in the Lake District. It was a record that stood for 11 years.

Campbell's health gradually failed him and he died in the little market town of Reigate in Surrey after a series of strokes in 1948. In this most dangerous era of record-breaking, he was one of the few daredevils who died of natural causes. His standing in the pantheon of speed kings is without equal and he was awarded the Segrave Trophy twice. He was inducted into the International Motorsports Hall of Fame in 1990 as perhaps the greatest land speed record holder in history.

RECORDS

Date	Venue	Car	Speed
September 25, 1924	Pendine Sands, Wales	Sunbeam	146.16mph / 235.22kph
July 21, 1925	Pendine Sands, Wales	Sunbeam	150.87mph / 242.80kph
February 4, 1927	Pendine Sands, Wales	*Blue Bird II*	174.88mph / 281.44kph
February 19, 1928	Daytona Beach, USA	*Blue Bird III*	206.96mph / 333.05kph
February 5, 1931	Daytona Beach, USA	*Blue Bird*	246.09mph / 396.03kph
February 24, 1932	Daytona Beach, USA	*Blue Bird*	253.97mph / 408.73kph
February 22, 1933	Daytona Beach, USA	*Blue Bird*	272.46mph / 438.48kph
March 7, 1935	Daytona Beach, USA	*Blue Bird*	276.82mph / 445.47kph
September 3, 1935	Bonneville Salt Flats, USA	*Blue Bird*	301.13mph / 484.60kph

ABOVE Campbell at the wheel of Blue Bird K3 on Lake Maggiore in 1937

LEFT Blue Bird K4 at speed on Coniston Water

Chapter 13

Sir Henry O'Neil DeHane Segrave

Born: September 22, 1896, Baltimore, USA | **Died:** June 13, 1930, Windermere, Cumbria, England

Henry Segrave was born to an American mother and Irish father in Baltimore. He was raised in Ireland but was schooled at Eton and served with the infantry and as a fighter pilot in the Royal Flying Corps during the First World War. He was recruited to the RAF in 1919 but resigned due to injuries sustained during the conflict – he'd been shot fighting for a supposedly abandoned trench and also survived a plane crash – and transferred to the administrative wing of the service. After the war, he helped design and build a twin-engined monoplane for luxury touring.

He pestered Talbot for a drive at the 1921 Brooklands 200 Miles and promptly won the race. He then won the French GP at Tours and also took the chequered flag at San Sebastian (both in a Sunbeam), thereby becoming the first British driver to win a grand prix in a British car. After another win at Miramas, he decided to concentrate on breaking the land speed record. (He'd always boasted that he would drive a car at more than 200mph.)

In 1926, he claimed the record for Britain in a modified Sunbeam Tiger on Southport Sands in Lancashire at a speed of just over 150mph. He then backed up his earlier conviction and became the first person to drive at more than 200mph when he took his 1,000-horsepower Sunbeam to Daytona Beach in the United States. His final re-

cord (231mph) came at the same venue in the beautiful *Golden Arrow* in 1929, a feat for which he was knighted. This car remains the least used in the history of the land speed record as it was retired immediately after the record run with only 18.74 miles on the clock.

As a keen boat racer, Segrave travelled straight to Miami to take on American national hero Garfield Wood who

ABOVE Segrave's crew work on the Golden Arrow before his record attempt at Daytona Beach in 1929

hadn't lost a race on water in nine years. Segrave inflicted an embarrassing defeat on his rival when Wood's steering cable failed, and he soon returned to England to try to reclaim the outright world water speed record from his nemesis. He promptly built a beautiful seven-tonne 4,000-horsepower craft and christened her *Miss England II*.

Segrave took the boat onto Winder-

mere in June 1930 and raced through the measured mile at 96.41mph. On the return leg with the wind and current in his favour, he reached 101.11mph but he didn't yet know he'd broken the record and believed the boat had more to give. This dashing hero of motor-racing's golden age was killed when *Miss England II* struck a submerged log and capsized on her third run having already set a new record at 98.76mph. Segrave was knocked unconscious in the accident but came round in hospital for long enough to be told that he had broken the record. In so doing, he became the first man to hold both the land and water speed records simultaneously. His engineer, Victor Halliwell, also died in the crash, but mechanic Mike Willcocks was thrown clear and survived with just a broken arm.

The Segrave Trophy was named in his honour and is presented annually to the Briton (or member of the Commonwealth) who accomplishes the greatest achievement in the air or on

SIR HENRY O'NEIL DEHANE SEGRAVE

ABOVE Segrave at the controls of Miss England II

RIGHT The Segrave Trophy

land or water. Past winners of the trophy include Amy Johnson, Malcolm Campbell, Geoff Duke, Stirling Moss, Donald Campbell, Bruce McLaren, Jackie Stewart, Roger Clark, Barry Sheene, Richard Branson, Mike Hailwood, Richard Noble, Nigel Mansell, Carl Fogarty, Colin McRae, Damon Hill, Andy Green, Joey Dunlop, Adrian Newey, John Surtees and Lewis Hamilton.

RECORDS

Date	Venue	Car	Speed
March 21, 1926	Southport, Lancashire	Sunbeam *Ladybird*	152.33mph / 245.15kph
March 29, 1927	Daytona Beach, USA	Sunbeam *Mystery*	203.79mph / 327.97kph
March 11, 1929	Daytona Beach, USA	*Golden Arrow*	231.45mph / 372.46kph

Chapter 14

John Godfrey Parry-Thomas

Born: April 6, 1884, Wrexham, Wales | **Died:** March 3, 1927, Pendine Sands, Wales

John Parry-Thomas was educated at Oswestry School and later studied engineering at college in London. He then joined Leyland Motors to design commercial vehicles and teamed up with automotive engineer Reid Railton to bring the luxury Leyland Eight to market. He took the car round Brooklands and, having won 38 races in five seasons in a variety of cars, decided to try his hand at record-breaking as this would bring the company wider recognition.

He bought a car from the estate of Count Louis Zborowski after the racing driver was killed at the Italian Grand Prix at Monza. He rebuilt the Higham Special, improved the aerodynamics and fitted a 27-litre Liberty V12 aero engine that used a Benz gearbox and was chain driven.

He made several test runs in 1925 but, without the financial backing secured by Campbell or the factory team of Henry Segrave, he couldn't get the engine to produce enough power. He couldn't afford a new Napier Lion engine to increase the output but he still took the car to Pendine Sands in 1926 and had a crack at the record. To everyone's surprise, he smashed Segrave's time through the measured mile by two seconds and raised the land speed record from 152.33 to 169.30mph. Despite poor conditions and soft sand bogging the car down, he raised it again the following day by another two miles per hour. Campbell sent a message of congratulation and immediately began preparing *Blue Bird* to reclaim the record.

Parry-Thomas decided to accept the challenge and he modified the car further

JOHN GODFREY PARRY-THOMAS

during the winter before returning to the seven-mile stretch of beach in the spring of 1927. Campbell had just broken his record from the previous year and he was determined to be the first man to run at more than three miles a minute. With help from Shell and Dunlop, his team prepared the car, christened *Babs*, for a run on the beach. After a short warm-up, Parry-Thomas started his first timed run but his rear suspension collapsed and the car rolled over and slewed round towards the sea. Parry-Thomas had been partially decapitated, possibly by a flailing drive chain, and the car was also on fire. To retrieve his body

RECORDS

Date	Venue Car	Speed	
April 27, 1926	Pendine Sands, Wales	Higham Special *Babs*	169.30mph / 272.45kph
April 28, 1926	Pendine Sands, Wales	Higham Special *Babs*	171.02mph / 275.22kph

from the wreck, two of the crew had to break his legs.

The coroner's verdict was accidental death and Parry-Thomas was buried at Saint Mary's Church in Byfleet, Surrey, near the track at Brooklands. The car was buried in a hole on the beach but it was eventually salvaged by Owen Wyn Owen in 1969. He spent the next 15 years restoring the car and *Babs* is now exhibited periodically at the Pendine Museum of Speed.

Parry-Thomas's team, which included engineers Ken Thomson, Ken Taylor and Reid Railton, went on to work for Malcolm Campbell and helped build the *Blue Bird* series of cars used in land speed record attempts in the 1930s.

BELOW Babs at Brookland

Chapter 15

Charles Raymond 'Ray' Keech

Born: May 1, 1900, Coatesville, Pennsylvania, USA | **Died:** June 15, 1929, Tipton, Pennsylvania

Ray Keech was born into a farming family but he was never tempted to join the family business and deliver milk to the locals using a horse and cart. He spent his spare time working on cars instead, and soon earned a reputation for racing trucks while working for the town mechanic. He eventually graduated to dirt-track racing and by 1927 he'd set several records at Langhorne.

Keech moved his family to Philadelphia the following year and he came to the attention of wealthy manufacturer Jim White. White wanted to have a crack at the land speed record so he convinced Keech to help him build a triple-Liberty-aero-engined 36-cylinder 81-litre monster to wrestle the title from the British. Keech was honoured to be asked to drive as it might lead to greater standing in the racing community, so the team relocated to Daytona Beach in Florida. However, he immediately became aware of the dangers of land speed record-breaking when a water hose fractured and sprayed him with boiling water. He then had to cope with a fire in the front engine and fumes in the cockpit as he began his second run.

One of the timekeepers announced

RECORD

Date	Venue	Car	Speed
April 22, 1928	Daytona Beach, USA	*Spirit of Elkdom*	207.55mph / 334.02kph

afterwards that their equipment had malfunctioned so they couldn't verify a new record. Rather than waste his energy berating the officials, Keech simply got back into the car and completed another run at the record speed of 207.55mph. Such was the trauma of the attempt that he vowed never to run the car again.

When Segrave recaptured the record for Britain in the beautiful *Golden Arrow*, mechanic Lee Bible was tempted by the prospect of sporting immortality so he asked to run the White Triplex. Jim White agreed but Bible was killed when he lost control during deceleration and the car ploughed into the sand dunes. Photographer Charles Traub was also killed in the accident.

Keech decided that record-breaking was simply too dangerous so he set his sights on winning the world's most prestigious motor race: the Indianapolis 500. In May 1928 he was on his way to victory when a fuel line split and burned his legs. He returned to the hallowed Brickyard the following year and managed to avoid a huge pile-up that claimed the life of Bill Spence. A record audience of 160,000 then saw him win the 500 at an average speed of nearly 100mph. He was six minutes ahead of his nearest rival and only 12 of the 33 starters finished the race. Keech took home a cheque for $40,000 and was showered with praise from the global racing fraternity.

Sadly, he wouldn't live long enough to enjoy the accolades. Two weeks later he was killed at the notorious Altoona Speedway when he swerved to avoid a slower car and struck the guardrail. He was thrown from the car in the accident but was then hit by another car as he tried to crawl to safety on the infield.

Chapter 16

Captain George Edward Thomas Eyston

Born: June 28, 1897, Oxfordshire, England | **Died:** June 11, 1979, London, England

Engineer and inventor George Eyston's career was interrupted by the First World War but he served with distinction with the Dorset Regiment and the Royal Field Artillery. In 1917, he was awarded the Military Cross for:

"Conspicuous gallantry and devotion to duty. He rendered most valuable service when carrying out reconnaissance under heavy fire. On several occasions he went forward under heavy shell- and machinegun fire. He carried out his duties with great courage and determination, and was able to obtain most valuable information."

He returned to Trinity College in 1919 and began entering car races across the continent. He enjoyed great success with Aston Martin and Bugatti and won the 1921 and 1926 French Grand Prix. He also invented the Powerplus Supercharger and fitted it to his *Magic Midget* MGs.

He set several speed-endurance records at Brooklands before deciding to have a tilt at the land speed record at Bonneville. His first car, *Speed of the Wind*, was underpowered for an outright record attempt so he set an average for 24 hours at 140.52mph. Over the next two years, Ab Jenkins, John Cobb and Eyston traded endurance records, while Malcolm Campbell raised the outright record to more than 300mph.

Eyston then decided to build a stream-lined car with multiple aero engines for an assault on Campbell's record. The

result was *Thunderbolt*, a seven-tonne behemoth using a pair of Rolls-Royce V12 engines, of which Campbell's *Blue Bird* only used one. Each 36.5-litre powerplant developed 2,350 horsepower and drove four wheels through a single axle (four more wheels were allied with a twin axle). The chassis was covered with polished aluminium but the car wasn't as aesthetically pleasing or as streamlined as John Cobb's *Railton Special*. It also had a large rear tailfin and hydraulic air brakes. For later record attempts, Eyston used ice to cool the engine as the radiators created too much drag.

He made his first record attempt

CAPTAIN GEORGE EDWARD THOMAS EYSTON

ABOVE Eyston's Thunderbolt is wheeled out of the workshop

at Bonneville in November 1937 and reached an average speed over the two legs of 311.42mph, comfortably faster than Campbell's *Blue Bird*. It seemed as though rival John Cobb might break the record immediately but Cobb's

Railton wasn't ready until the following year. With both men on the salt flats in 1938, the first big duel for the land speed record began.

Eyston made minor aerodynamic adjustments to *Thunderbolt* and raised

RECORDS

Date	Venue	Car	Speed
November 19, 1937	Bonneville, USA	*Thunderbolt*	311.42mph / 501.16kph
August 27, 1938	Bonneville, USA	*Thunderbolt*	345.49mph / 556.01kph
September 16, 1938	Bonneville, USA	*Thunderbolt*	357.50mph / 575.31kph

the record to 345.49mph but Cobb then became the first man to exceed 350mph on land. Eyston knew his car had a tiny reserve of power but he had to modify the air intake to reduce drag. He also had to wear a respirator as exhaust fumes and toxic particles from the new disc brakes filled the cockpit. He took the car onto the flats the following day and broke Cobb's record by four miles per hour (357.50mph). The record stood for nearly a year, whereupon Cobb raised it beyond *Thunderbolt*'s capability. With the outbreak of the Second World War imminent, Eyston's fabulous car never ran again. It was eventually destroyed by a fire in a warehouse in New Zealand. *Speed of the Wind* was also destroyed, this time by an enemy bomb that struck the works in Willesden where it was stored.

Despite being rivals, Eyston and Cobb enjoyed an excellent professional relationship: while Eyston was working for Castrol he was also an adviser to Cobb's water speed record project. During the war, he worked for the Ministry of Production but he finally returned to record-breaking at Bonneville in 1954. Driving a supercharged MG EX-179, he and co-driver Ken Miles set eight international and 28 national records. Eyston also experimented with fitting radios to aircraft in 1912, was captain of the Trinity Boat Club at Cambridge and raced motorboats in his spare time. This racing legend eventually became director of Castrol and was one of the few record-breakers to die from natural causes in 1979.

BELOW Thunderbolt on the salt flats at Bonneville

Chapter 17

John Rhodes Cobb

Born: December 2, 1899, Esher, Surrey, England | **Died:** September 29, 1952, Loch Ness, Scotland

John Cobb made his money as a director of his father's fur broking company, and this allowed him to compete in prestigious races at Brooklands near the family home in Esher. In 1935, he used the technical know-how gleaned from years spent preparing cars to break the lap record at the iconic track in a Napier Railton. This was considered one of the great achievements in racing at the time as it had previously been held by Sir Henry 'Tim' Birkin in a Bentley Blower and Oliver Bertram in an eight-litre Barnato-Hassan Bentley. Cobb's average speed of 143.44mph still stands as the track fell into disuse after the Second World War.

Cobb was determined to bring the record-breaking technology of his racing cars to ordinary road vehicles, and he helped develop safer tyres and better grades of oil that could be passed on by manufacturers to consumers. He then set about building a car for an attempt on the land speed record. He approached noted designer and engineer Reid Railton and the pair shoehorned two 1,300-horsepower W12 Napier Lion aero engines (donated by female powerboat racer Marion Carstairs) into a steel chassis. Railton dealt with the problem of delivering this power to the wheels by splitting the axles and making the car four-wheel-drive. The body was designed using the National Physics Laboratory's wind tunnel and the sleek car was eventually

christened the *Railton Mobil Special*.

Cobb took the car to the Bonneville Salt Flats in 1938 to have a crack at Eyston's 345mph world record. He immediately raised the mark to 350mph, the first time the milestone had been breached. Eyston fought back the following day, however, and took the record to 357mph. This lifted it out of Cobb's reach until the following year when he returned having improved the Railton's aerodynamics. A few days before the outbreak of the Second World War, Cobb reclaimed the record from Eyston with a two-way average of nearly 370mph.

He served as an RAF and Air Transport Auxiliary pilot during the conflict but he returned to record-breaking immediately afterwards. Both Britain and the USA had made great technological leaps during the war and men like

Donald Campbell were now suggesting powering a new breed of cars with jet engines. Cobb decided that with a few more modifications the Railton could break the 400mph barrier before any of these new cars could be built.

On September 16, 1947 he fired up the *Railton Mobil Special* for a final tilt at the record. His first run yielded a speed of 385.65mph, good enough for the record but some way short of the magic 400. On his return run, the Railton dug deep and delivered a world first: 403.15mph. The two-way average of 394.20mph may have been just shy of his target but Cobb was the first man to exceed 400mph on land.

He briefly entertained thoughts of making another run in the hope that it was also over 400mph but the car was at its limit and he decided discretion was the better part of valour. (The car had already set 5- and 10-mile endurance records at 327 and 270mph respectively.) Instead, Cobb returned home and started work on a jet-powered boat that he hoped would deliver the water speed record.

Crusader was a Railton-designed trimaran powered by a de Havilland Ghost gas turbine turbojet. Cobb took the craft to Loch Ness in September 1952 and began preparing for an attempt on American Stan Sayres's 178.50mph mark set in *Slo-Mo-Shun* in July. By the end of the month, Cobb was confident

RECORDS

Date	Venue	Car	Speed
September 15, 1938	Bonneville, USA	Railton	350.20mph / 563.58kph
August 23, 1939	Bonneville, USA	*Railton Special*	369.74mph / 595.02kph
September 16, 1947	Bonneville, USA	*Railton Mobil Special*	394.20mph / 634.39kph

of reclaiming the record for Britain but, when travelling at around 210mph having just been through the measured mile, *Crusader*'s bow plane collapsed and the rest of the craft disintegrated as it nosedived into the loch. Cobb's body was recovered shortly afterwards but he was already dead. His average speed through the mile had been 206.89mph but the record required a return run so it stayed with the Americans.

Cobb's *Railton Mobil Special* is on display at the Thinktank Science Museum in Birmingham. *Crusader*'s remains were recovered from the bottom of the loch in 2002.

BELOW Cobb's jet-powered boat Crusader

Chapter 18

Donald Malcolm Campbell, CBE

Born: March 23, 1921, Kingston, Surrey, England | **Died:** January 4, 1967, Coniston Water, England

Donald was born to the greatest land speed record holder of them all, Sir Malcolm Campbell, and his second wife, Dorothy Evelyn Whittall. He grew up travelling the world as his father claimed nine land and four water speed records, and he soon developed his own taste for speed. He went to Seaford and Uppingham schools and would have flown with the RAF during the Second World War had he not suffered a crippling bout of childhood rheumatic fever.

He joined Briggs Motors in Thurrock as a maintenance engineer but waited until after his father's death (New Year's Eve 1948) before entering the race for the land speed record. He asked his father's engineer, Leo Villa, to help him design and build a series of cars and boats. It was almost as if he'd been waiting for the right moment to succeed Malcolm and then exceed his achievements.

Campbell first went after his father's water speed record. He dusted off *Bluebird K4* but couldn't match Malcolm's 141.74mph from 1939. He returned to Coniston Water again in 1950 but while he and Villa were testing the boat American Stan Sayers raised the record to 160mph, which was beyond *Bluebird*'s capability. Undeterred, Campbell took *Bluebird* back to his workshop and re-engineered her into a three-point hydroplane with twin cockpits. The new design reached 170mph only to suffer structural failure, probably after strik-

ing a submerged railway sleeper, before being wrecked. Campbell's misery was compounded when Sayers raised the record again to 178mph. He then had to face opposition from John Cobb's turbojet hydroplane, *Crusader*.

However, Cobb was killed on Loch Ness in 1952 when *Crusader*'s bow plane failed. Campbell resolved to bring the record back to Britain in Cobb's memory, so he asked Villa and Ken Norris to build him a jet-boat using 3,500lbs of thrust from a Vickers Beryl turbojet. Campbell promptly set seven water speed records in *Bluebird K7* between July 1955 at Ullswater and December 1964 at Lake Dumbleyung in Australia

(he'd been on the continent setting the world land speed record and decided to break both records in a calendar year, the first and so far only man to do so).

Campbell's land speed record bid was not without its problems, however. Ken and Lew Norris designed *Bluebird CN7* in the latter part of 1956. The Proteus-powered car used a turbine to drive all four wheels and it had a potential top speed of 500mph. By the spring of 1960, the 4,500-horsepower car was ready for a shot at John Cobb's 394mph record set back in 1947. The team travelled to Bonneville and gradually increased the speeds during test runs but Campbell lost control on the sixth pass and

ABOVE Campbell
was lucky to survive
Bluebird's high-speed
crash in 1960

crashed at 360mph. He was seriously injured and the car was destroyed, but he vowed to rebuild *Bluebird* and return to take the record.

Bonneville was eventually ruled out as the salt was in poor condition, but Campbell soon heard about Lake Eyre in Australia. It hadn't rained for nine years and the salt was perfectly smooth for 20 miles. The rebuilt car had only completed a few low-speed tests when storms washed out the 1962 attempt. Breedlove then drove his jet-powered tricycle *Spirit of America* to 407mph at Bonneville. It may not have conformed to the FIA's regulations, but in the eyes of the public Breedlove was now the world's fastest man.

Lake Eyre was still partially flooded in 1964 but Campbell ignored the risks and raised the official land speed record to 403.10mph after two courageous runs in poor conditions. As *Bluebird* had reached a peak speed of nearly 450mph on one pass, he was disappointed not to have broken Breedlove's unofficial record but the FIA still recognised Camp-

bell's achievement. When he added the water speed record on New Year's Eve, friends and relatives hoped he would retire from record-breaking.

Campbell had loftier goals, however. He commissioned the Norris brothers to design a land speed record car that could break the speed of sound, and he also set his sights on being the first man to reach 300mph on water. His first ambition was outlined with characteristic confi-

BELOW Campbell returned to Lake Eyre in 1964 and claimed the last wheel-driven land speed record in Bluebird

dence: "In terms of speed on the Earth's surface, my next logical step must be to construct a *Bluebird* car that can reach Mach 1.1. The Americans are already making plans for such a vehicle and it would be tragic for the world image of British technology if we did not compete in this great contest and win. The nation whose technologies are first to seize the 'faster than sound' record on land will be the nation whose industry will be seen to leapfrog into the 1970s or '80s. We can have the car on the track within three years."

To raise awareness about the rocket car, Campbell publicised the water speed attempt and fitted *Bluebird K7* with a lighter and more powerful Bristol Orpheus engine developing 4,500lbs of thrust. He took the modified boat to Coniston in November 1966 but initial trials were fraught with problems and he couldn't approach his existing mark of 276mph. More modifications to the fuel pump allowed Campbell to use full power so he waited for the weather to settle.

The morning of January 4, 1967

dawned bright and clear. Campbell was extremely superstitious but he ignored the fact that he'd drawn the Ace and Queen of Spades at cards the night before. This was the same combination drawn by Mary, Queen of Scots the night before she was beheaded. Campbell muttered at the time: "Someone in my family is going to get the chop. I pray to God it's not me but, if it is, I hope I'm going ruddy fast at the time."

He powered through the measured kilometre on his first run at 297mph, a whisker short of his target. Speculation has arisen about what happened next as Campbell usually stopped to refuel. However, he simply turned the boat around and began his second pass, which smoothed out once he'd passed the turbulence created by his water brake. At 700 metres from the beginning of the kilometre, he opened the throttle and was soon tearing across the lake at around 328mph. It's possible the boat began to tramp when he encountered his own wake but it's equally likely that the problematic Orpheus flamed out due to excessive vibrations as the sponsons struck the choppier water and caused a sudden deceleration. As the boat caught

OPPOSITE TOP
Campbell built a model of Bluebird Mach 1.1 in 1964

OPPOSITE BOTTOM
Donald Campbell with Leo Villa in Australia in 1964

BELOW Bluebird K7

DONALD MALCOLM CAMPBELL, CBE

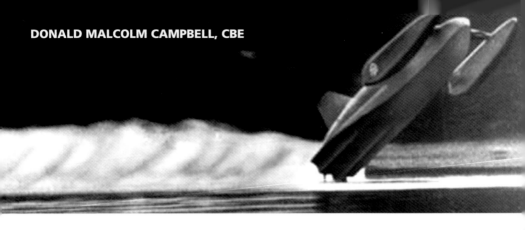

ABOVE Bluebird K7 leaves the water during the fatal crash

RIGHT Donald Campbell

its own wash, ground effect took over and the bow lifted. *Bluebird* then took to the air, almost completing a full somersault before smashing into the lake and disintegrating. Campbell was killed instantly and the world lost a British speed king.

Navy divers found the remains of *Bluebird* the following day but Campbell's body wasn't recovered until 2001. *K7* was eventually salvaged and restored by the Bluebird Project and may run low-speed demonstration trials on Coniston Water in the near future.

RECORD

Date	Venue	Car	Speed
July 17, 1964	Lake Eyre, Australia	*Bluebird* CN7	403.10mph / 644.96kph

Chapter 19

Craig Breedlove

Born: March 23, 1937, Los Angeles, California, USA

Craig Breedlove was born to special-effects supervisor Norman and his wife Portia, a studio dancer who worked with Fred Astaire and Ginger Rogers. He grew up building and modifying cars from the age of 13 and, three years later, when he was legally allowed to drive, he began drag-racing them in the Mojave Desert. He soon recorded a speed of 154mph in a supercharged Ford hotrod. Having visited the Bonneville Salt Flats, he decided to return at the age of 20 with a streamlined Oldsmobile, which he ran at 236mph.

While working for the Douglas aircraft company in his early 20s, he studied structural engineering, which gave him a solid foundation in design and metalworking, two of the skills he'd

RIGHT Craig Breedlove with Spirit of America

steering gremlins that compromised its high-speed control so Breedlove added a vertical stabiliser and an adjustable front wheel and returned to the salt flats the following year.

In the autumn of 1963 he reached 388mph on his first run, but he was only using 90% of the car's power. On his return run, he upped the thrust to 95% and clocked 426.43mph, a two-way average of 407.45mph. Cobb's mark had at last been broken, and the land speed record was returning to the USA for the first time since 1929. Or so Breedlove thought. As the car didn't have four wheels, and none of its three wheels were powered by the engine, the FIA excluded it from the record books. The governing body for world motorcycles accepted it as an outright speed record instead. Donald Campbell then took *Bluebird* to Australia and upped the wheel-driven record to 403.10mph, which was perilously close to Breedlove's top speed. The American was also under pressure from fellow hot-rodders Art and Walt Arfons, who had also built rival jet cars (*Green Monster* and *Wingfoot Express* respectively). In October 1964, the brothers upped the record to 434mph.

Breedlove roared back with a two-

need when building his record-breaking jet cars. In 1959 he began working on a new car, the three-wheeled *Spirit of America*, that he hoped would challenge John Cobb's outright land speed record of 394mph. Although the wheels weren't powered by the jet engine, Breedlove didn't give much thought as to whether his car was legal in the eyes of the FIA. He just wanted to be the fastest man on Earth. He even extended his house so that the build could be completed at home.

Power came from a military surplus J-47 turbojet producing 5,000lbs of thrust. The engine was originally used in the air force's F-86 Sabre but Breedlove picked it up for just $500 and by 1962 he was ready for a crack at the 15-year-old mark. However, the car developed

way average of 469mph on October 13. He then raised the record to 526mph two days later – the first time 500mph had been reached – but his brakes and parachutes both failed during the long deceleration phase and Breedlove lost control. *Spirit of America* skidded for nearly five miles, eventually colliding with a telegraph pole, leaping a low bank and nose-diving at around 200mph into a deeper section of the lake that was still swamped. Breedlove managed to escape from the wreck before it sank, but it was clear that the car had made its last run.

(Having climbed out, Breedlove memorably muttered: "And for my next trick, I'm going to set myself on fire.")

Spirit's 526mph was good enough to see off Walt Arfons and Tom Green with the *Wingfoot Express* team but it wasn't enough to outrun Art Arfons in the *Green Monster*. When Art made a final run late in October, he reclaimed the record at 537mph. By the end of the year, the FIA had introduced a new category for jet- and rocket-powered cars so Campbell's old *Bluebird* record was finally rendered obsolete. No wheel-

ABOVE Breedlove was lucky to survive a 675mph crash in Spirit of America Formula Shell

driven or piston-engined vehicles have held the outright record since, although Don Vesco did reach 470mph in his *Turbinator* in 2001 and he's aiming for 500+mph in 2016.

Breedlove salvaged *Spirit of America* and donated it to the Chicago Museum of Science and Industry. He then began work on a new car, *Spirit of America Sonic 1*, which he hoped would claim the record back from Arfons and take it out of his rival's reach. The car used a much more powerful GE J-79 engine from an F-4 Phantom fighter-bomber. By November 1965, Breedlove was ready so he took the car onto the salt flats and posted a two-way average of 555mph but the car had plenty in reserve so, two weeks later, he tried to raise the record again. The first run yielded 593mph and the return was slightly faster, although Breedlove felt the car was at its limit as

the run was extremely dicey. Timekeeper Joe Petrali eventually handed him a piece of paper with 600.601mph written on it. Breedlove wasn't sure if this was the speed from the second run or the two-way average but Petrali simply smiled and clapped him on the back. It was an astonishing record that would stand for five years. The car was eventually outclassed by Gary Gabelich's *Blue Flame* and Richard Noble's *Thrust 2* so Breedlove donated it to the Indianapolis Motor Speedway Hall of Fame Museum. (Petrali's son Dave would later manage the timing station for *Thrust SSC*'s runs in 1997.)

Breedlove then took a lengthy sabbatical from record-breaking but, when he learned of Noble's plan to go supersonic, he returned to the sport he'd graced. In 1992, he began work on a new challenger, *Spirit of America Formula Shell*. John Ackroyd's eye-catching ve-

hicle was more than 40 feet (12 metres) long and was powered by an upgraded J-79 developing 23,000lbs of thrust.

In 1996, Breedlove took the car to Nevada's Black Rock Desert in the hope of beating Noble's 633mph average in *Thrust 2*, which had been set back in 1983. His project lacked major sponsorship investment so his support team was small. The crew monitoring the timing equipment also provided some of the meteorology data, for example. A spotter in a light aircraft overhead then fed this information to Breedlove.

Breedlove gradually took the car up to around 650mph but the weather was deteriorating quickly. He needed to make a second run within an hour to set a new record so he waited for the weather data to be relayed to the cockpit. His spotter gave him news of a crosswind reaching 'one-five', which Breedlove interpreted as 1.5mph, well within the safety limits. However, the observer had actually meant 15mph with gusts to 25mph, which was beyond the car's design limits.

Breedlove immediately accelerated to begin his second pass and he entered the measured mile at around 675mph. The car was then caught in the crosswind and flipped onto its side. Breedlove tried to regain control but the car cut a wide U-turn across the desert, narrowly missing a Winnebago before eventually coming to rest. The ever-fortunate Breedlove was unhurt after yet another dramatic incident but his record attempt was over for the year.

He returned in 1997 but his engine was damaged on an early run and the car could only reach 676mph, a speed that would have been good enough to claim a new record had Wing Commander Andy Green not set a supersonic record of 763mph in *Thrust SSC* in October.

ABOVE Breedlove scorches across the playa at high speed

CRAIG BREEDLOVE

Ever the gentleman, Breedlove had allowed the *Thrust* team to use his facilities when his project stalled and he was one of the first on the scene to congratulate Richard Noble's outfit on a remarkable world first. Had Breedlove not suffered mechanical failure, early season rains, and a lack of test data regarding taking *Spirit of America Formula Shell LSRV* supersonic, he may have reclaimed the record for the USA but he graciously conceded defeat to the British.

In Green, he sees a kindred spirit as they are both men who are prepared to put their lives on the line chasing records. Breedlove knew that *Thrust SSC* was extremely difficult to drive and had a tendency to leap 50 feet to the left at around 500mph. He doubts that any other driver could have controlled the car in that situation, let alone hold his nerve to push on to nearly 800mph, and he believes that *Thrust*'s record was

mostly down to Green's skill and bravery. Breedlove realised his car probably couldn't match the new record so he sold it to adventurer Steve Fossett. Fossett planned to have a crack at the speed of sound but he was killed in 2007 when his light aircraft came down in the Sierra Nevada Mountains.

Breedlove's recent quests for speed were sandbagged by a lack of sponsorship and funding. It seemed that the American public had also lost interest in land speed record-breaking. However, he is not one to accept his lot and in 2010 he unveiled models of a new vehicle, *Supersonic Spirit of America 3*, which he hopes will yield a top speed in excess of 1,000mph and bring the land speed record back to the USA for the first time since 1983. At 78, Breedlove is too old to drive the car but he will manage the project and few would bet against one of the greatest land speed record holders.

RECORDS

Date	Venue	Car	Speed
August 5, 1963	Bonneville, USA	*Spirit of America*	407.45mph / 655.71kph
October 13, 1964	Bonneville, USA	*Spirit of America*	468.72mph / 754.33kph
October 15, 1964	Bonneville, USA	*Spirit of America*	526.28mph / 846.97kph
November 2, 1965	Bonneville, USA	*Spirit of America Sonic 1*	555.48mph / 893.96kph
November 15, 1965	Bonneville, USA	*Spirit of America Sonic 1*	600.60mph / 966.55kph

Chapter 20

Tom Green

Born: Born: 1931, Chicago, USA

Part-time stock-car racer Tom Green was working as an engineer for a torque-wrench manufacturer when he met Walt Arfons at a trade fair in Indiana in 1962. Arfons was more interested in racing mechanics and Green was studying aerodynamics, but within 10 minutes they were plotting an assault on the two versions of the land speed records that were held by Donald Campbell and Craig Breedlove.

Green went to work on the car's design, although he changed the original tricycle layout to four wheels to comply with the FIA's regulations for outright records. He spent most of his time lowering the drag coefficient, reducing the frontal area by narrowing the vehicle's track and installing a military surplus

ABOVE Wingfoot Express is made ready to roll at Bonneville

ABOVE Wingfoot Express 2 was powered by 25 JATO rockets

ment to allow them time on the Bonneville Salt Flats so they approached Goodyear Tyres. Green wowed executives with his knowledge of aerodynamics and correctly predicted that Nathan Ostich's challenger, the jet-powered *Flying Caduceus*, would only reach 360mph, whereas Campbell's *Bluebird* might just reach 400mph. Goodyear were suitably impressed and agreed to the pair's proposal, so the team repaid the compliment by calling the car *Wingfoot Express* after Goodyear's winged-foot logo (*Bluebird* would eventually hit 440mph in poor conditions

J-46 Westinghouse jet engine. He then built a cockpit just behind the front axle, covered it with an acrylic canopy and mounted the two rear wheels on outriggers for stability.

Arfons and Green still needed invest-

but Green and Arfons already had the funding in place by then).

Walt was supposed to drive the car but he suffered a suspected heart attack when it ran out of control during a test. He then damaged the tendons in

RECORD

Date	Venue	Car	Speed
October 2, 1964	Bonneville, USA	*Wingfoot Express*	413.20mph / 664.98kph

his hand while they were unloading the rebuilt car at Bonneville so Green was chosen to drive instead. In the autumn of 1963, he and Arfons arrived at Bonneville and began with several low-speed runs but, despite never having driven at more than 130mph, Green was soon posting speeds approaching 300mph. The car was suffering from the stresses and strains of running on salt, however, and crystals engorged by the engine sent it out of balance, derailing the pair's attempt and allowing Breedlove to take the record at 407mph.

In October 1964, three teams convened on the salt flats: Craig Breedlove was driving *Spirit of America*, while Walt's half-brother Art had brought *Green Monster* to the party. *Wingfoot Express* was expected to challenge but the engine seemed short of power and Green couldn't get much above 300mph. Despite being in direct competition for the record, Art Arfons suggested opening the clamshell engine exhausts to glean more power from the afterburner. Green made the adjustment and also modified the bodywork around the air intake.

The results were spectacular and Green immediately posted a run of 406mph. To break Breedlove's record,

he needed to make a return pass within the hour at least three miles per hour faster. It was late in the day and there was no time to refuel so Green used a short approach and gave the engine max power only two miles from the timing lights. *Wingfoot Express* roared through the measured mile at 420.07mph on her return run, yielding a record two-way average of 413.20mph.

Having helped with his half-brother's record attempt, Art Arfons was now determined to beat *Wingfoot Express* in the *Green Monster*. Green's record therefore only lasted three days but, despite the car having plenty in reserve, he decided not to run again and retired from competitive auto racing. Walt Arfons continued running the team alone and he returned to Bonneville with *Wingfoot Express 2* in 1965. The new car was powered by 25 solid-fuel jet-assisted take-off (JATO) rockets and reached a peak speed of 605mph in 1965. However, the rockets couldn't be changed in time for return runs and the car couldn't maintain these speeds through the measured mile so it was redundant as a land speed record vehicle. By the end of the season on the salt flats, Breedlove had raised the record to more than 600mph anyway.

Chapter 21

Arthur Eugene 'Art' Arfons

Born: February 3, 1926, Akron, Ohio, USA | **Died:** December 3, 2007, Springfield, Ohio, USA

Art's father Tom was born in Greece but he came to the USA in 1912 and later married Bessie who was half Native American. She already had three children: Walt, who was 10 years older than Art; Dale, who was eight years older; and sister Lou who was 18 months older. Tom ran a feed mill in Akron and all the brothers learned engineering while maintaining it. Art later joined the navy and was soon serving as a mechanic in the Pacific. He fought during the Second World War but was discharged in 1948.

When Tom died in 1950, Walt and Art channelled their energy into drag racing and they were soon building their first cars. Somewhat surprisingly, their mother endorsed them, even when they ended up competing against one another in their *Green Monster* series of dragsters. (The cars got their name when stadium announcer Ed Piasczik introduced one of them as a 'green monster' in 1952.) The brothers were soon building drag racers of note, and *Green Monster* 6 became the first car to break 150mph in the standing quarter mile. *Green Monster 11* then beat drag-racing's biggest name, Don Garlits, with a 191mph run.

In the early 1960s, the brothers became fascinated with bringing the land speed record back to America. Art's first serious attempt was at Bonneville in a car modelled on John Cobb's *Railton Special* but he could only manage 314mph in

the aircraft-engined *Anteater*.

Arfons returned to the salt flats in 1962 with a primitive jet car but the 8,000-horsepower *Cyclops* fell 60mph short of Cobb's 394mph record. The design of the cockpit and air intake severely limited the top speed but the car did employ an aerodynamic wing to keep it on the ground. Arfons then bought an ex-military General Electric J-79 turbojet for just $600. Despite the manuals being classified – and therefore unavailable – he completely rebuilt the engine with a four-stage afterburner delivering 17,500lbs of thrust.

Both brothers and Craig Breedlove

ABOVE Art Arfons's Green Monster jet car

LITTLE BOOK OF **LAND SPEED RECORDS**   **91**

early October. Having helped Walt with his car's teething problems, Art took *Green Monster* to 434mph a few days later but his record only lasted a week before Breedlove reclaimed it at 469mph in *Spirit of America*. Two days later, Breedlove thought he'd put the record beyond the Arfons brothers with an average of 526mph but Art wasn't to be outdone and he delivered a new record of 537mph at the end of October. With racing over for the season, Breedlove retired to lick his wounds, although he would return in 1965 with the much more powerful *Spirit of America Sonic 1*. He promptly reclaimed the record at 555mph but

faced off in the desert in 1964. Breedlove held the record at 407mph but Walt's *Wingfoot Express*, driven by Tom Green, added six miles per hour in

RECORDS

Date	Venue	Car	Speed
October 5, 1964	Bonneville, USA	*Green Monster*	434.03mph / 698.48kph
October 27, 1964	Bonneville, USA	*Green Monster*	536.71mph / 863.73kph
November 7, 1965	Bonneville, USA	*Green Monster*	576.55mph / 927.84kph

Arfons replied with a superb 577 in the *Green Monster*. This turned out to be the car's last run as it blew a tyre during deceleration, and Breedlove then put the record out of sight at 601mph.

Arfons still believed *Green Monster* could capture the record, however. He returned to Bonneville in 1966 but could initially only manage 554mph. Then, on November 17, while travelling across the salt at 610mph, a wheel bearing seized and the car crashed. He eventually built another vehicle but sold it to racing driver Slick Gardner at his wife's insistence. He never went for the land speed record again and concentrated instead on competitive tractor pulling, at which he enjoyed great success. He also occasionally exhibited his jet cars at events across the US.

Tragedy struck during an exhibition run in Dallas in 1971, however. Arfons lost control of his jet-powered dragster *Super Cyclops* when a tyre burst. His passenger and two spectators were killed in the crash, although Arfons only sustained minor injuries. It was his last competitive event.

In 1989 he returned to Bonneville to test several high-speed bikes and cars but he had another crash at 350mph. Two years later, handling problems in the desert forced Arfons to retire from all forms of motorsport. This unlimited drag-racing record-holder, champion tractor puller and three-time land speed record-holder was inducted into the Motorsports Hall of Fame just before his death in 2007.

OPPOSITE Arfons redesigned the nose and added an aerodynamic wing for stability at higher speeds

BELOW Arfons retired from competitive racing when the Super Cyclops crashed and killed three people in 1971

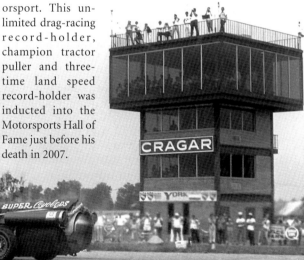

Chapter 22

Gary Gabelich

Born: August 29, 1940, San Pedro, California, USA | **Died:** January 26, 1984, San Pedro, California, USA

Gary Gabelich was born to Croatian parents on August 29, 1940 in San Pedro, California. He began racing his father's Pontiac while still at school and won his first competition. He backed this up by taking the world's first jet dragster race at 250mph. In 1959, he apparently took a jet car to more than 350mph on the Bonneville Salt Flats, although this story is difficult to verify.

He worked as a delivery driver for Vermillion's Drug Store but still lived in Long Beach with his parents. He then signed up with North American Rockwell and, over the next nine years, he graduated to become a part-time test subject for the Apollo Program, not as an astronaut but as a physical and mental performance monitor. He also volunteered to skydive alongside (and film) the first landing capsules as they were dropped from 30,000 feet.

In his spare time, Gabelich satisfied his appetite for speed in funny cars on drag strips but Rockwell issued an ultimatum when they learned about his dangerous side interests. So Gabelich gave up his job in pursuit of the land speed record. It was a crucial moment in his life because Reaction Dynamics, a company formed by Pete Farnsworth, Ray Dausman and Dick Keller, had recently developed a hydrogen peroxide-powered rocket dragster and they were looking for a driver. *The Blue Flame* was a 37-foot, two-tonne, 58,000-horsepower vehicle that was built in Milwau-

ABOVE Gary
Gabelich's Blue Flame

kee and sponsored by the American Natural Gas Industry. The team initially approached Craig Breedlove but he wanted too much money. Their second choice, drag racer Chuck Suba, agreed terms but was killed shortly afterwards. This left the way clear for Gabelich and he signed up immediately.

The team wanted to run at Bonneville in September 1969 but the car couldn't be prepared in time so they had to wait until the following year. Gabelich's first run yielded a disappointing 426mph, well short of Breedlove's 601mph record set five years earlier. The team worked day and night to fine-tune the car and Gabelich reached 609mph on the first of two mandatory runs on October 15, but a mechanical problem prevented him making a return run within the hour. A week later he scorched through the measured mile at 621mph but the team again failed to turn the car around in time to make a second run. Finally, on October 28, Gabelich and *The Blue Flame* averaged 617.60mph on the first run and 627.21 on the second to set a new land speed record of 622.41mph. The peak speed was around 650mph and the kilometre record was raised to

630.39mph (1,014.51kph).

Gabelich said afterwards that he thought *The Blue Flame* might be capable of 750mph, which would have been enough to break the sound barrier, but Reaction Dynamics had no plans to run the car again and Gabelich went back to drag racing. His right hand was severed in an accident in 1972 but the operation to reattach it was a partial success and he continued racing until 1980. He also spent a fair amount of time on the water and won the American Power Boat Association Blown Fuel and Gas National Drag Boat Championships in 1968 (becoming the first person to win them both in the same year). The following

season he became the first pilot to reach 200mph in a drag boat, although he almost gave up boat racing when his machine disintegrated at 180mph on Turlock Lake in California in 1975.

Gabelich was killed in 1984 when his motorcycle hit the side of a truck in Long Beach. He died three hours later at San Pedro Hospital at the age of only 43. He had just seen his land speed record broken by Richard Noble in *Thrust 2* at the Black Rock Desert in Nevada and was apparently planning to reclaim the title for the United States. In 1985, Long Beach City Council named a park in his memory. *The Blue Flame* is now permanently exhibited at the Auto & Technik Museum in Sinsheim, Germany.

RECORD

Date	Venue	Car	Speed
October 28, 1970	Bonneville, USA	*The Blue Flame*	622.41mph / 1,001.64kph

Chapter 23

Stan Barrett

Born: June 26, 1943, Bishop, California, USA

S tan Barrett was a former lightweight Golden Gloves champion and Hollywood stuntman who worked on films like *When Time Ran Out, Smokey and the Bandit* and *The Cannonball Run*. The latter two were directed by stunt co-ordinator Hal Needham, a man with a fascination for speed and record-breaking. In the mid-1970s he contemplated building a car to break the land speed record.

With sponsorship from Budweiser, designer Bill Fredrick, a consultant to the aerospace industry, built a rocket car that resembled *The Blue Flame*. He called the vehicle the *SMI Motivator* but

RIGHT Stan Barrett inside the Budweiser Rocket's cockpit

ABOVE It will always be debated whether the car actually broke the sound barrier. The weight of evidence suggests not, but Barrett's bravery and skill should never be doubted

it was slightly Heath Robinson in design and didn't undergo extensive wind-tunnel testing. He soon decided to paint it red and add the Budweiser name to the flanks to generate publicity.

Barrett had been introduced to car racing by Paul Newman in the early 1970s so he was chosen to drive. When the *Budweiser Rocket* first ran at Bonneville, Needham immediately realised it didn't have the power or fuel capacity to complete return runs through the measured mile. Rather than completely rebuild the vehicle to challenge for the official record, Needham decided to add

the 12,000-horsepower booster from a Sidewinder missile and aim instead at the sound barrier, which would be a unique world first. It didn't matter that they couldn't claim the land speed record as the sound barrier presented a much tougher goal. Budweiser were so impressed with his plan that they offered the team a million-dollar bonus if Project Speed of Sound was successful.

Needham poured $800,000 into the project and fitted the missile in the tail above the car's 48,000-horsepower rocket engine. On the morning of December 17, 1979, Barrett squeezed into the tiny cockpit beneath the tailfin. The speed trap, which was just 52.8 feet (1/100th of a mile) long, was two miles down the track as this was calculated to be where the car's fuel would run out. The team even called in retired General Chuck Yaeger, the first man to break the speed of sound in air in the *Bell X-1* rocket plane in 1947, to help verify the run. Yaeger also procured the air force's ground-radar tracking systems to monitor the car's top speed.

The temperature was cold at 20 degrees Fahrenheit so the speed of sound was 731.90mph (the speed is a function of temperature and pressure so the prevailing weather played an important role in the attempt). Barrett ignited the hybrid rocket and activated the Sidewinder motor 14 seconds into the run, but the car ran out of fuel just short of the timing trap, by which time its speed had dropped to around 660mph. All eyes turned to the air force radar equipment but it had recorded the speed of a truck in the distance and returned a hit of 38mph. Undaunted, the team set about analysing the car's accelerometer data and, after eight hours, proclaimed that the car had reached a peak speed of 739.67mph or Mach 1.01 for a fraction of a second. And

this is where the controversy boiled over.

Chuck Yaeger believed the car had gone supersonic because the rear wheels became airborne for around 200 metres (660 feet) due to the shockwaves forming under the car at Mach 0.9. However, it's far more likely that as the car lost nearly a tonne in weight from burning fuel, lift generated from the rear suspension struts sent the car 10 inches into the air. It was miracle that Barrett didn't crash. Also, no photos exist of any shockwaves forming, except around the rear wheels, which is completely unlike the supersonic runs of *Thrust SSC* in which shockwaves were visible to the naked eye. Needham's team has never officially released data from the air-speed indicator and the in-car accelerometer so the *Budweiser Rocket*'s top speed can't be independently calculated or even accurately estimated. No sonic boom was heard by spectators at Rogers Dry Lake or in the surrounding area, which is again at odds with what was observed by the *Thrust SSC* team in 1997. *Thrust*'s booms rattled windows in Gerlach several miles away and spectators also heard them above the noise of the Rolls-Royce turbofan engines.

Perhaps the final nail in the coffin is

STAN BARRETT

ABOVE Hal Needham managed Project Speed of Sound but he didn't release the team's data before his death in 2013

that Needham continued to deny access to all the data from the run and rarely rebutted the letters accusing him of falsifying his claim. And no governing body has ever recognised a speed of greater than Mach 1. Indeed, Needham's insistence that his own team be the sole arbiters of the attempt rather than an independent and impartial body smacks of arrogance and creates room for doubt over the claimed speed. He died of cancer in 2013 at the age of 82 so the full story may never be known.

For those with a love of speed and the mystique surrounding breaking the sound barrier, it is a great shame that Barrett and the *Budweiser Rocket* didn't achieve their goal. This incredibly brave man was undoubtedly the fastest man on Earth at the time, and may have remained so for nearly 20 years. Without the crucial data, however, the car's top speed can only be estimated, and the available evidence suggests it reached nearly 700mph.

RECORD ATTEMPT: SPEED OF SOUND

Date	Venue	Car	Speed
December 17, 1979	Rogers Dry Lake, USA	*Budweiser Rocket*	660+mph / 1060+kph

Chapter 24

Richard James Anthony Noble, OBE

Born: March 6, 1946, Edinburgh, Scotland

Richard Noble's quest for speed began at the age of six when he was on a family outing to Loch Ness. As his father drove their Hillman Minx along the loch, Richard noticed John Cobb's jet boat Crusader preparing for an attempt on the world water speed record. He soon became fascinated by Cobb and his land speed records, even though most of his contemporaries idolised Sir Malcolm Campbell.

Noble was educated at Winchester College and he then qualified as a pilot. He was also a keen businessman and entrepreneur who was prepared to take personal and financial risks: he helped develop the ARV Super 2 light aircraft

RIGHT Richard Noble with Thrust 2

RICHARD JAMES ANTHONY NOBLE, OBE

and backed the Atlantic Sprinter, a contender for the Blue Riband, the mystical reward for the fastest Atlantic crossing by boat. Despite humble beginnings both projects seemed to be viable, although financial troubles soon derailed them. He then founded Farnborough F1 air taxis to enable businessmen to bypass the expensive and inefficient transport system around London but that project also stalled.

Noble's real passion lay with speed, however, and he began a lifelong affair with the record in the 1970s when he decided to build a jet car. He started out with only £1,500, of which most came from the sale of his Triumph TR6, and

he christened the basic jet-powered vehicle Thrust 1. He knew the first incarnation would never break the land speed record but he hoped to learn how to control such vehicles on Britain's runways. If testing was successful, he'd build Thrust 2 to promote the project and raise sponsorship money, and then Thrust 3 could try for the record.

Thrust 1's initial tests were promising but a wheel bearing seized at around 140mph on one run in the spring of 1977 and the car rolled three times. Noble was unhurt but the car was a write-off and he only made £175 after selling it for scrap. Incredibly, Noble found the finance for the second vehicle by October and he displayed Thrust 2 at the London Motor Fair to raise awareness of his record attempt.

Noble managed to install a Rolls-Royce Avon from a Lightning jet fighter into a chassis designed by John Ackroyd. The car resembled the Arfons brothers' Green Monster in that the cockpit was mounted on one side of the engine. Sponsors gradually came onboard and the project was progressing well by 1979. News of Stan Barrett's possible speed-of-sound run didn't faze the team as it wasn't sanctioned by any reputable

organisation – plus Gabelich and Breed-love gave it no credence whatsoever – and by 1981 the Thrust team were ready for their assault on Gabelich's record. They decided to go with accepted wisdom and run on the salt flats at Bonneville but the car's solid wheels couldn't cope with the salt and they only managed a 500mph run before the rains came. The team had insured themselves against the weather and the payout enabled them to return to Bonneville in 1982, but the weather was even worse and Thrust couldn't run at all. During the second trip, Noble had learned about the Black Rock Desert so the team headed there in 1983. It was the perfect venue for record-breaking and the team had soon cleared a 13-mile course across the playa. On September

ABOVE Noble's next land speed project was Thrust SSC

RICHARD JAMES ANTHONY NOBLE, OBE

years earlier. But Noble couldn't make a return run within the hour so the record stayed with the American.

He was also finding that Thrust was digging into the desert as the speeds increased. The extra downforce needed to be counteracted so that Thrust was lighter on her wheels so, on the advice of John Ackroyd and Craig Breedlove, the team raised the nose a fraction. The results were immediate: on October 4, Noble managed 624mph on the southern run and 642mph heading north, with a peak speed of a shade over 650mph. He'd finally wrestled the record back from the Americans. It later emerged that the car would probably have taken off at 660mph due to the team raising the nose, so they called time on the project at the right moment.

Noble channelled his energy into other interests until the end of the decade, but he then became aware of challenges to his record from the McLaren Formula 1 outfit as well as Breedlove. He immediately formed a team to assess the possibility of building a supersonic car, but it took

29, Noble roared down the track at 622.84mph, almost exactly the same speed as Gabelich had managed 13

RECORD

Date	Venue	Car	Speed
October 4, 1983	Black Rock Desert, USA	*Thrust 2*	633.47mph / 1,019.44kph

another five years before Thrust SSC was ready to take on Breedlove's Spirit of America Formula Shell in the Black Rock Desert (by then the McLaren challenge had faltered, as had Rosco McGlashan's Aussie Invader). Breedlove's car had crashed the year before and then its engines failed early on in the duel against Thrust SSC. Rather than walk away, Breedlove lent his support to the British team with characteristic generosity, and Noble's driver, RAF fighter pilot Andy Green, finally smashed the sound barrier in October 1997, exactly half a century after Yaeger had broken it in the air.

Noble again decided that he'd had enough of land speed record-breaking and in 2002 he vowed never to return to the sport. However, barely five years later, he and Green had joined forces once again to see off the challenge from the Americans. More teams gradually joined the hunt for a new land speed record, and Noble's Bloodhound SSC is now one of eight cars hoping to raise the record beyond 1,000mph.

OPPOSITE Noble also channelled his energy into the ARV Super 2 (top) and the Atlantic Sprinter (bottom), seen here as an artist's impression

BELOW Noble is now promoting the Bloodhound SSC project

Chapter 25

Andy Green, OBE

Born: July 30, 1962, Warwickshire, England

Andy Green was born in Atherstone but he went to grammar school in Kent and joined the RAF via a scholarship to Worcester College, Oxford, in 1980. Having graduated, he qualified as a fighter pilot on Phantoms and Tornados. He was then approached by Richard Noble and asked to try for a place on the *Thrust Supersonic* Car team. Noble had previously held the land speed record with *Thrust 2* but he now wanted the biggest prize in the sport: a supersonic record.

As Stan Barrett's heroic run in the *Budweiser Rocket* still hadn't been confirmed – the team refuses to this day to release all their accelerometer data – Green became one of many candidates pushing for the role of test driver with Noble's new project. As a fighter pilot he had all the skills required and he outperformed the other drivers so he was chosen to spearhead the *SSC* project.

Noble also drafted in Glynne Bowsher, Ron Ayers, Jeremy Bliss and John Ackroyd to design the car and, once it had been built, the team first headed for the Al-Jafr Desert in Jordan. Although they encountered many logistical and technological gremlins, they were confident enough to head to the Black Rock Desert in Nevada in the autumn of 1997 to mount a challenge on Noble's old record and then the sound barrier.

Thrust SSC's two afterburning Rolls-Royce Spey engines developed approxi-

mately 80,000 horsepower, although they had to propel the 10-tonne missile down the playa at more than 700mph. The team had to overcome myriad problems in the desert but Green finally broke Noble's 14-year-old mark on September 25, 1997. Although he managed 714mph, the sound barrier remained tantalisingly out of reach.

Three weeks later, Green overcame his fear once more – the car had a tendency to sideslip at around 500mph – and opened the throttles for one last run. Fifty years and one day after Chuck Yeager had become the first man in history to break the sound barrier in the *Bell X-1*, *Thrust SSC*'s shockwave echoed around the mountains and the nearby hamlet of Gerlach. His first run was 759.33mph but the team needed to make a second pass at the same speed or better within the hour to claim the world's first supersonic land speed record. This time the turnaround went without a hitch – they'd recorded two supersonic runs two days earlier but they were a minute outside the allotted hour – and the car hurtled through the measured mile on its return run in just 4.7 seconds. As another sonic boom

ANDY GREEN, OBE

home, JCB asked Green to head a project hoping to claim the diesel-powered land speed record, which had stood at 236mph (380kph) since 1973. The *JCB Dieselmax* was tested in the UK before being shipped to Bonneville in the summer of 2006. On August 23, 2008, Green broke the mark he'd set the previous day and raised the record to 350.09mph (563.42kph). For this achievement he was awarded the John Cobb Trophy by the British Racing Drivers' Club.

ABOVE Thrust SSC scorches to the world's first supersonic land speed record in 1997

OPPOSITE BOTTOM Green with a model of his next land speed record car

rumbled across the desert, the team erupted in triumph. Green's second run was Mach 1.024 and the record was his. He was immediately decorated with an OBE and he also received the Segrave Trophy.

Soon after the team had returned

Later in the year, Noble asked Green to drive his next land speed record car, *Bloodhound SSC*, which had a theoretical top speed of 1,050mph (1,690kph). The team are heading to South Africa for shakedown tests in 2015, and a record attempt could be made in 2016.

RECORDS

Date	Venue	Car	Speed
September 25, 1997	Black Rock Desert, USA	*Thrust SSC*	714.14mph / 1,149.30kph
October 15, 1997	Black Rock Desert, USA	*Thrust SSC*	763.07mph / 1,227.99kph

LEFT Green at the wheel of the record-breaking JCB Dieselmax

1,000 mph Supersonic Car
Inspiring the next generation

The Future of the
Land Speed Record...

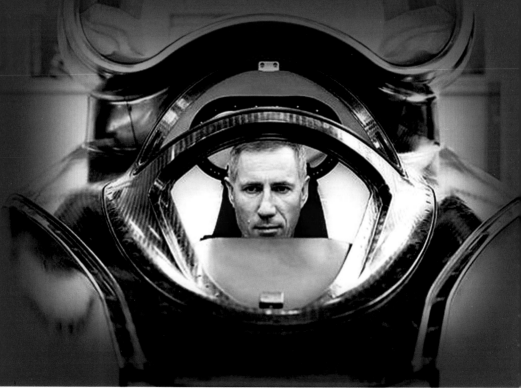

Chapter 26

Bloodhound SSC

In 2006, the team behind *Thrust SSC* – Richard Noble, Andy Green and Ron Ayers – got wind of a record attempt by American adventurer and entrepreneur Steve Fossett. He'd bought Craig Breedlove's old Spirit of America, which had crashed at around 675mph in 1996 and was then rendered obsolete during the duel in the desert with *Thrust SSC*, and was going to make small design and aerodynamic modifications to have a crack at Green's supersonic mark in 2008. Fossett was killed in a plane crash in 2007 but Noble's team, which now included Swansea University's College of Engineering with backing from the government, had already begun preparing to defend the record for Britain. They also wanted to promote British science, technology and engineering so they embarked on an ambitious tour of the country to bring their story to thousands of school children.

They promptly set themselves the target of reaching 1,000mph in an all-new car called *Bloodhound SSC*. They extended the target date for achieving this to 2016 as the Black Rock Desert in Nevada and the Bonneville Salt Flats in Utah weren't suitable for the new car. Instead, the team are in the process of creating a 12-mile track at the Hakskeen Pan in South Africa. It's worth bearing in mind that at top speed the car could cover 12 miles in 43.2 seconds, so the margin for error on a record attempt is painfully thin.

In fact it represents what might be the last land speed record in a history dating

OPPOSITE Green assesses the cockpit

back to 1898. Even if the cars of the future become more powerful and more aerodynamic, there aren't many places on Earth long enough or flat enough to run them. The car will use virtually all of the Hakskeen Pan during the acceleration, timed mile and deceleration phases so there's no room for a vehicle to travel much faster.

There is also the driver to consider. The reaction times necessary to steer the car at 1,000mph – or more than a quarter of a mile (1,466 feet) per second – are nearing the limits of what even a fighter pilot is trained for. Wing Commander Andy Green will once again control the vehicle, which will be able to accelerate to top speed in 42 seconds and will decelerate at 3g, but the RAF pilot doesn't have the safety net of an ejector seat that he would have in his Eurofighter. Any failure is likely to result in catastrophe, so safety

is the team's primary concern. The main problem facing them is how to keep the vehicle on the ground.

There are considerable aerodynamic challenges to overcome when taking a land vehicle to 1,000mph. Passenger aircraft are designed to take off at about 150mph but cars and boats can also generate lift, either by design or accident. It's quite common to see racing three-point hydroplanes flip and Donald Campbell famously lost control of *Bluebird K7* on Coniston Water in 1967. The boat's nose lifted out of the water and threw the craft into a somersault at around 300mph. It disintegrated on impact, killing Campbell and all but stopping future water speed record attempts. Indeed only a handful of people have ever been faster on water and Australian Ken Warby's record of 317.6mph has stood since 1978. Nearly 85% of all record attempts have ended in fatalities since 1940.

Technological developments have allowed drivers to raise the land speed record four times in the same period, although the faster the record becomes, the more difficult it is to beat. The first records were set in electric cars but internal combustion dominated for the next half century. Only after the advent of the jet age did speeds reach more than 500mph. To push up to and beyond the sound barrier, only jet and rocket power is suitable. However, at these speeds air resistance – not much of a factor at low speeds – becomes the crucial parameter. Only extremely powerful cars that have undergone rigorous aerodynamic testing can now hope to break the land speed record. These tests used to be conducted in wind tunnels but supercomputers now simulate the effects, crunch the numbers and display the results using computational fluid dynamics. They can also model shockwaves and turbulence in the vehicle's wake.

While working to resolve these issues, the *Bloodhound* team realised that the car's nose could be kept at a constant height above the ground by ensuring the net pressure generated by the airflow above it and underneath it remained neutral. The real problem would be keeping the rear of the car on the ground when subsonic and supersonic shockwaves formed around the outboard rear wheels and suspension housing. What may have seemed like a relatively simple problem took the team six months to solve and resulted in them designing a delta fairing that recently featured in the *Journal of Automobile Engineering*. The new design protects the underside of the vehicle from the high-pressure cushion around the rear wheels when the car exceeds the sound speed barrier. Without the new fairing, the car would take off at around 90% of the speed of sound.

Designing a twin intake duct to deliver a suitable airflow to the EJ-200 jet engine compressor across the entire speed range was also problematic so the team reverted to a single intake above the cockpit. The engine itself was based on the Rolls-Royce XG-40 and comes from a Eurofighter Typhoon. Although it produces around 120 kilo-Newtons (27,000lb/f), the car will also use a bespoke hybrid Nammo rocket with a supercharged Jaguar V8 to drive its oxidizer pump. With a total of 135,000 horsepower, *Bloodhound* will have more than six times the power of all the cars on a Formula 1 grid combined. The car will run shakedown tests in the summer of 2015 and a record attempt could be made the following year.

The British team are hoping that they will write the final chapter in the enthralling saga of the land speed record, but several other countries and teams will also be mounting a challenge on the record in the near future.

Chapter 27

The North American Eagle

The *North American Eagle* jet car is based on the military F-104 Starfighter that was used by the American air force from 1957 until 1970. The team under owner Ed Shadle includes Jessi Combs, who hopes to break Kitty O'Neil's female land speed record of 512.70mph (825.13kph) before pushing on to a maximum speed of around 800mph.

The project was announced in 2003 and their first tests were conducted in June 2004. The converted F-104 once served as a chase plane for the record-breaking *X-15* rocket plane and the SR-71 *Blackbird*. It retains the original air intake ducts but the wings have been clipped so it doesn't take to the air at high speed. At 13,000lbs (5,896kg) in weight and 56 feet (17.07m) from nose to tail, the *North American Eagle* is powered by a General Electric LM-1500 turbojet engine that has been modified to produce 52,000 horsepower. At idle,

BELOW Jessi Combs prepares for another test run

the powerplant consumes 35 gallons of fuel per minute (151 litres) but under full afterburner it guzzles 80 gallons per minute (350 litres).

The Federation International de l'Automobile (FIA) states that for the vehicle to be considered a 'car' it must run on four wheels, so the team chose solid aluminium to reduce the rolling weight and eliminate the problems of rubber tyres at the speed of sound. This also allows the driver to pilot the ground-based fighter rather than having to drive it.

In 2004, the team headed to the Black Rock Desert in Nevada and made several runs of up to 400mph but the project then seemed to stall, possibly because their design top speed of 808mph fell short of the target proposed by the Brit-ish *Bloodhound* team.

However, in October 2013, Combs broke Lee Breedlove's 1965 four-wheeled mark of 308.51mph with a run of 392.95mph. The team now have the backing of Microsoft so the project is back on track and they are hoping to complete another series of tests in 2015.

ABOVE The North American Eagle land speed record challenger

BELOW The car runs a shakedown test

Chapter 28

Aussie Invader 5R

The *Aussie Invader* series of land speed record cars are the brainchild of Australian drag racer Rosco McGlashan. An adventurer at heart, McGlashan built the first *Aussie Invader* to challenge Richard Noble's 633mph *Thrust 2* record from 1983. In March 1994, he took the first incarnation onto the salt flats of Lake Gairdner in South Australia but he only reached 500mph.

The following year, McGlashan returned to the lakebed for another attempt in a modified car called *Aussie Invader II*. However, the salt was in poor condition after a spell of bad weather and McGlashan veered off course at 600mph and struck the timing equipment. The car was completely destroyed and McGlashan was lucky to walk away uninjured. His third car was built to challenge Andy Green and Craig Breedlove for the first supersonic land speed record but the salt was again

in poor condition and the attempt had to be abandoned. While a fourth car was being prepared, McGlashan drove a rocket-powered go-kart at 253mph (407kph) to claim a class record at the same top speed as a Bugatti Veyron.

The land speed record-challenging *Aussie Invader 5R* is based on *The Blue Flame* and the *Budweiser Rocket* and has a theoretical top speed in excess of 1,000mph. Boasting a 0-1,000mph time of 20 seconds, the vehicle is 15 metres (49 feet) long and weighs nine tonnes. It's powered by a single rocket engine producing 62,000lbs of thrust, which equates to around 200,000 horsepower, so it's 50% more powerful than the *Bloodhound*. The air pressure on the vehicle at top speed will be approximately 12 tonnes per square metre (one tonne per square foot) so the body must be extremely durable, rather like a submarine.

McGlashan is determined to break the record on home soil so he's been scouting more locations in Queensland in case Lake Gairdner is unsuitable. If his enormous team of volunteers can finish preparing the car and clearing a track, the indomitable Aussie could have a crack at the record in 2015 or 2016.

OPPOSITE Rosco McGlashan with Aussie Invader 5R and Aussie Invader III

ABOVE An artist's impression of Aussie Invader 5R

Chapter 29

Fossett LSR

BELOW The Fossett
LSR was based on Craig
Breedlove's Spirit of
America Formula Shell

Amerian businessman, record holder and adventurer Steve Fossett became interested in breaking the land speed record in 2006. He'd been enthralled with the duel in the desert between Craig Breedlove's *Spirit of America* and Andy Green's *Thrust SSC*, so he decided to buy Breedlove's car after it crashed at nearly 700mph. Fossett spent several years developing the project but he was killed in 2007 when his light aircraft crashed in the Sierra Nevada Mountains.

A new buyer was found and the team behind project has a realistic goal of 850mph with the current General Electric J-79 engine developing 18,400lbs of thrust. Other than the engine, however, most of the car has now been updated. It may look like a tricycle but it has two narrow front wheels reducing drag and providing stability. The suspension, brakes, steering, parachute-delivery systems and wheels have all been renewed with the hope of exceeding the current supersonic land speed record.

Chapter 30

Sonic Wind and Imagine LSRV

The *Sonic Wind* project is the brainchild of Waldo Stakes. His mission is to design, construct and pilot the most advanced, powerful and fastest ground vehicle in history. The car will be powered by an XLR-99 rocket engine with a composite combustion chamber that propelled the North American *X-15* rocket plane to the air speed record of 4,519mph (7,273kph) in 1967, a mark that still stands for manned aircraft. The car is most likely to run on ice, while a separate project, the *Imagine Land Speed Research Vehicle*, will try for the conventional record in the American desert.

Stakes began modifying motorcycles at the age of 14 and he also developed a hobby building homemade rockets. By the age of 20 he was designing aerodynamic body shells for rocket-powered dragsters that set records across the

BELOW Sonic Wind's rocket is tested in the desert

USA in the 1970s. He then moved to California and started work on his first rocket-powered unlimited land speed record vehicle. He eventually came up with the idea for *Sonic Wind*, a bipropellant-rocket ice racer that was designed, aero tested and built on the edge of the Mojave Desert. The project was funded from his income as a contractor and the car was built with the help of only two friends: Ken Mason handled the propulsion system and Larry Hayes built the car itself.

Stakes was also a regular at El Mirage and Bonneville and he worked on several land speed motorcycle streamliners and various other class cars. He was voted into the SCTA club of Land Speed Racers and continued working on vehicles that set more than 30 land speed records in many SCTA classes. The 15 years he spent at Bonneville allowed him to learn the intricacies of land speed vehicles and their dynamics.

Now known as 'Mr Landspeed', he is the CEO of Land Speed Research Vehicles and co-owner and builder of the *Sonic Wind* and *Imagine LSRV* rocket cars. The latter has a unique aerodynamic design and a tremendously powerful MR-40K rocket engine, which is a modified Rocketdyne LR-105 that was originally used in the Atlas intercontinental ballistic missile. The engine produced more than a million horsepower when it powered John Glenn's Mercury capsule to an escape velocity of 17,500mph in 1962.

The current *Imagine LSRV* configuration will allow the car to reach a speed in excess of Mach 2 (1,400mph) on land, faster than any jet fighter at low altitude. The team has the option to add larger fuel tanks that could raise the car's theoretical top speed to Mach 3, about the same as the SR-71 *Blackbird* at high altitude.

Stakes considers the land speed record to be an art that takes a lifetime to master. He lives in the Ord Mountains in the high desert of Southern California and his primary goal is to bring the land speed record back to the United States after 32 years in British hands.

OPPOSITE TOP A model of the Imagine LSRV

OPPOSITE BOTTOM Waldo Stakes

BELOW Imagine LSRV takes shape

The Bullet Project

The Bullet Project was founded by Paul Noone, a car builder from Perth in Western Australia. He aims to design a vehicle called the *RV-1*, which is a 30-foot, three-tonne, kerosene-powered rocket car with a potential top speed of 1,000mph. A much larger car was originally considered but the team are working to a budget and a smaller vehicle could make a record attempt on the nine-mile Lake Gairdner Salt Flats in Australia rather than travel all over the world testing at venues like the Black Rock Desert or Bonneville.

Rocket propulsion was chosen for its power-to-weight ratio and because the large air intake for a jet would cause too much drag on a small vehicle. The *RV-1* will burn two tonnes of liquid oxygen and kerosene, providing up to 50,000lbs of thrust. This will be controlled by the driver so that maximum speed is achieved within the measured mile on both runs. As it could be prohibitively expensive to make live runs at gradually increasing speeds, the acceleration curves will be plotted before-hand. When allied with

the aerodynamic results from computational fluid dynamics experiments, the team should be able to plot the car's performance accurately without having to make too many runs.

The car itself will have its fuel chambers, cockpit and nitrogen tanks separated by sturdy bulkheads to minimise the risk of explosion. It will have four wheels to avoid the stability problems suffered by several previous record cars, including the *Budweiser Rocket* and *Spirit of America*, and will be mainly constructed of carbon fibre with rolled magnesium. The centre of gravity will be towards the front of the car, and small fins and ground-effect grooves will keep it on the ground. The wheels are perhaps the most difficult part to design as they will be rotating at more than 10,000rpm and generating 50,000g at the rim. Only the outer rims of the 30-inch wheels will rotate and the car will have an internal suspension system. The wheels will only be eight inches wide as the team

hope they will plane across the salt rather than digging grooves into the lakebed.

As with all the LSR projects, the most important concern is driver safety. Noone's team decided that they could incorporate a separate capsule for the driver that could detach in much the same way as the cockpits on racing hydroplanes. However, as these safety cells only release after an accident has initiated, the team decided to create a hybrid system that drew on the ejection seat design from most fighter aircraft. Compressed air rams will fire the capsule to safety should an accident occur and the vehicle pitches or rolls beyond predetermined limits. It will then be slowed using a ballute (balloon/parachute) braking system to protect the fireproof and blast-resistant capsule from impact damage.

Progress has been slow but steady and the team hope to make their first test runs in 2016.

Chapter 32

Jet Black

In the history of the official land speed record, only four countries have had the honour of having the world's fastest car: Belgium, France, the United States and England. With their Rolls-Royce Avon-powered *Jet Black*, a team from New Zealand led by businessman Richard Nowland is aiming to steal the record from under Aussie Rosco McGlashan's nose. Having unveiled the car in October 2011, it is in the early stages of development but testing could begin in the US or Australia in late 2015 or early 2016.

If the single jet engine delivering 18,000lbs of thrust performs as expected, the team will add two rocket motors delivering another 40,000lbs of thrust – for a total equating to approximately 85,000 horsepower – to reach more than 1,000mph. The car will be driven by RNZAF pilot Wing Commander Stephen Hunt, a veteran of several operational tours in Iraq and Bosnia, where he flew GR7 Harriers. Richard Roake is the team's aerodynamicist, while former *Thrust* employee Glynne Bowsher has designed the forged-aluminium wheels. The car is 13 metres long and weighs around five tonnes with a full fuel load.

Nowland is prioritising an outright land speed record but he is also promoting Kiwi science, technology, engineering, business and innovation. He believes that the car and the organisation behind it can bring New Zealand know-how to a global audience. Rather than name a specific speed, Nowland believes the car is capable of more than *Bloodhound* or *Aussie Invader*.

BELOW An artist's vision of Jet Black at top speed

Chapter 33

Supersonic Spirit of America 3

Craig Breedlove is one of the land speed record's most enduring personalities. He was the first person to set two-way records at more than 400, 500 and 600mph and he has now set his sights on the 1,000mph barrier. Having survived a spectacular 675mph crash in *Spirit of America* in 1996, and then failing to beat Andy Green and *Thrust SSC* in 1997, Breedlove decided that he was too old to be piloting a new vehicle that he hoped would make its first runs in 2013-14.

Breedlove has designed the car, *Supersonic Spirit of America 3*, but Neil Roberts, a chassis engineer with Honda Performance Development, will run the overall project. Roberts also worked as an aerodynamicist for Jim Hall's Indy Car team and as a structural engineer for Grumman Northrop Aviation. Mark Zweig will drive the beautiful machine. He holds the diesel truck speed record but he's also a skilled mechanic and an F-16 fighter pilot.

So far, the team only have computer renderings and scale models of the vehicle but it's likely to be powered by a pair of General Electric J-79 jet engines from S&S Turbine. Together, they will produce approximately 40,000lbs of thrust and deliver a top speed in excess of 1,000mph. The chassis will be built from a welded steel space-frame but the nose will be a composite structure similar to those on F1 or Indy Cars. The cockpit survival cell is a carbon-fibre monocoque that will detach in the event of an accident, while a parachute will immediately deploy to slow it down and reduce impact forces. The wheels will be made from carbon fibre to reduce weight and increase strength. The car's onboard brain will sense deviations in yaw, pitch and roll and it will make minor adjustments to power and trim settings before Zweig even realises there could be a problem.

The team will build two identical cars so that one can be used for promotion and to attract sponsors, and it can also step in should one crash or develop me-chanical problems. Breedlove hopes to build them within two years and he will then start looking for sponsorship. He has always maintained that Bonneville is where the cars should run but the salt flats have degraded recently and prob-ably aren't suitable. Neither is the Black Rock Desert, so it's likely the team will have to look elsewhere. Lake Gairdner in Australia and the Hakskeen Pan in South Africa are possible alternatives.

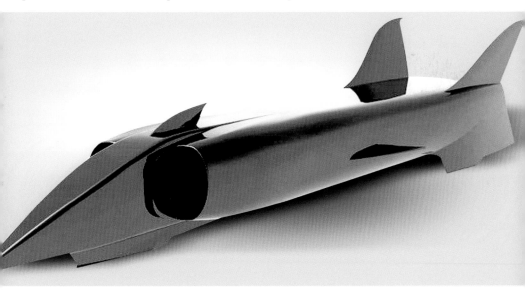

BELOW Breedlove's proposed design for Supersonic Spirit of America 3

Design & Artwork: ALEX YOUNG

Published by: DEMAND MEDIA LIMITED

Publisher: JASON FENWICK

Written by: LIAM McCANN